LEARN HOW TO BUILD YOUR TREASURE CHEST

Reginald A. Allen

Learn How to Build

Your Treasure Chest

Sail to a Safe Harbor and financial security

Reginald A. Allen

LEARN HOW TO BUILD YOUR TREASURE CHEST
Sail to a Safe Harbor and financial Security

"This is a wonderful and straightforward introduction to the basic principles and strategies for retirement planning. It is an invaluable resource for young and old, one I wish I'd had years ago. I have given a copy to each of my children."
— Billie J. Mendoza, Administrative Assistant, Walt Disney Imagineering

"This book is an excellent introduction to some smart techniques for building an energetic retirement fund, making especially clear the significance of compounding over time and the power of time to effect growth."
— Glen Pfeifer, Ph.D.

"Reg Allen's highway map to financial future is paved with excellent advice at every turn. Your Treasure Chest is a very readable journey into the Retirement Future for all who would avoid the many potential pitfalls and misadventures that Mr. Allen describes. Filled with up to date and hard-earned wisdom, I commend this book to all those hopefuls entering or already upon the road to a secure and successful retirement."
— John Rutter, Esq.

"Mr. Allen offers exponential insight into the vast array of simple investment opportunities available in a saving deficient society."
— Jody Westfall, Assistant Vice President, Bank Branch Manager

"This booklet is an invaluable guide to help prepare for a more secure financial future. For those people just beginning their working careers it's an excellent stimulus to establish early the habits necessary for systematic accumulation of an estate for retirement. The text develops in a very clear and logical manner, featuring informative illustrations, graphs and glossaries. Read it often and follow it faithfully."
— Larry Phipps, retired school teacher

""Over 50 years ago, in college, I majored in Finance and Investments. After reading this basic book in a brief few hours, I realized I would have accumulated far more wealth over my lifetime, using the author's simple approach, than all of the more sophisticated methods with which I had experimented. Mr. Allen brings an engineer's mind to this otherwise complex and arcane subject, resulting in an east-to-comprehend, A-to-Z elegance. Imagine how practical this book would be in a high school Finance class, encouraging this younger generation to prepare for what surely will be a retirement no longer funded by our rapidly expiring Social Security program. This book belongs in the Christmas stocking of every high school and college student."
— Bob Holman, Business Broker Consultant

Learn How to Build

Your Treasure Chest

Sail to a Safe Harbor and financial security

Reginald A. Allen

FANTASTIK-ACT
PUBLICATIONS
Lynnwood, Washington

Notice

This publication is designed to provide accurate and authoritative information in regard to the subject matter covered. It is sold with the understanding that the publisher is not engaged in rendering legal, accounting, or other professional service. If legal advice or other expert assistance is required, the services of a competent professional person should be sought.

— From a declaration of principles jointly adopted by committee of the American Bar Association and a committee of publishers.

Learn How to Build Your Treasure Chest
Sail to a Safe Harbor and Financial Security
Written and illustrated by Reginald A. Allen

Printed in the USA at BookMasters, Inc. Ashland, Ohio

ISBN 978-0-9815751-0-0

First published in 2010 by Fantastik-Act Publications

Library of Congress Control Number: 2008905961
Allen, Reginald A.

Learn How to Build Your Treasure Chest
Sail to a Safe Harbor and Financial Security / Reginald A. Allen

Includes bibliographic references and index.

ISBN 978-0-9815751-0-0
1. Dividend reinvestment
2. Exponential saving
3. Buying and selling stocks
4. Account management
5. Investing
6. Income taxes

To my wife Norma,
my grandchildren
Janell, Jessica, Christa
Veronica, Jared, Evan
and Johnathon, and also
to my greatgrandsons
Brandon, Christopher
and Logan.

"If you don't know where you're going
you end up somewhere else."

Paul Mariner

Super English football player & coach.

Contents

The Author on 14,494 ft., Mt. Whitney

Reginald Allen – man of all seasons – is or has been a plumber, electrician, electronic engineer, master gardener, artist, mountaineer, canoe builder, radar technician, soccer referee and coach, inventor, and member and outings leader in the Sierra Club for forty years and now a writer, illustrator and publisher.

Acknowledgments

I would like to thank my English nephew Michael Gibbs for his InDesign guidance, my friends: Norm Grossman, Barbara Masterson, Glen Pfeifer, Ed Dos Remedios and Bob Rinehart for their help and encouragement, Thanks also to Tracy Salter for editorial assistance and copy editing.

Statement

You can't just sit there and wait for people to give you that golden dream. You've got to get out there and make it happen for yourself. –Diana Ross

Prologue

There was a time when I believed leading Boy Scouts or Sierra Clubbers on backpack outings would instill in them a love for the wilderness and turn them towards conservation. At least, that's what I fooled myself into believing. Later I came to acknowledge my true purpose was the joy of being in the mountains, free from urban restrictions, At the time, I thought it worthwhile to teach those young people survival skills: how to light a fire in the snow, make pennyroyal tea or find the sweetest gooseberries. Much older now, I realize it was unlikely they would ever starve in a wilderness; they were more likely to suffer from malnutrition after reaching their elder years.

If I had realized those facts at the time I was gallivanting around the High Sierras, instead of wilderness survival skills I would have taught the financial survival skills I have learned since 1988. That was the occasion my employer gave me a $600 check, for being awarded a patent. I had little financial knowledge the, only a desire to invest in stock that would go towards providing an income when I retired. So I handed my money to Duanne Remsnyder, a discount broker in La Jolla, California, and asked his advice. I was not aware at that time that discount brokers don't give advice. Duane just picked up his newspaper and said, 'WD-40 pays dividends, you could go with them." My check paid for his fee and 20 shares of WD-40 at $27.75 per share.

Unfortunately, the WD-40 company does not allow dividend investment, so for the past 20 years my quarterly dividends have been deposited in a Credit Union account. Since then WD-40 stock split, now I have 40 shares, each worth $34.85, so the value of my stock is $1,394. Some people would consider a capital gain of 251% to be a satisfactory investment, yet since the 25¢ dividend only provides a quarterly income of $10; it does little towards my retirement, so I look upon it as a failure.

By the time I received my second patent award I had discovered many companies have dividend reinvestment plans.

After studying Charles Carlson's directory I was undecided between two energy supply companies; the dividends offered by *Enron* were the highest and recommended, but intuitively I believed *Atmos* to be safer. And on April 26, 1993 I purchased 15.35 shares at $26.19. Since then I have continuously invested small amounts, typically $25 to $50, for additional shares. We all know what happened to *Enron*, so I was fortunate in my intuitive choice. I now own 294 shares of Atmos and my quarterly dividends at the end of 2008 was $94.31.

It's unfortunate our youngsters leave high school without being taught the financial skills to manage their earnings. I had zero investment know-how two decades ago and made many mistakes. It's my hope that by passing on what financial wisdom I have gathered since then to the thousands of bank tellers, therapists and other low-income people who are stressed because they can see no way of saving, they will learn how to create and manage a Treasure Chest for their retirement.

This book can also fill a concealed need for middle class couples who have lived together for twenty or more years and find it difficult to talk of a future when one of them will be single and live on half their income. By regularly putting a small amount into a Treasure Chest, it will go a long way to ensure that the survivor will not be poverty stricken as well as lonely. It is not another investment book and although buying stock is required, it's not done with the objective of creating a large equity from which you can draw money during retirement. Instead it helps you slowly build a portfolio of stocks from which you will receive regular dividends during your retirement, and do so without reducing your equity. To make learning the financial terms simpler for those people whose knowledge of stock market terminology is little or none, I have introduced the words slowly, a few at a time in each chapter and added a glossary at the end of each chapter,

Middle-age and older people who have no computer savvy, can easily manage their Treasure Chest with paper and pencil. The middle-age boomers who only use their computers for games and word-processing, can exercise their neural system as they learn to manage their Treasure Chest by creating a software spreadsheet.

Chapter 1

Retirement Reality

Many young people find reality television depicting survival in a contrived situation to be entertaining, but for countless older people, survival after retirement is a looming reality that in each day pushes them closer to a financial chasm they can see no way of evading. How can They? The Social Security safety net which in 2006 supplied two-thirds of all people over 65 with more than half their income, is broken; and just like Humpy Dumpy, in 2008, none of the President's cronies and none of the President's jesters could put piggy together again.

For many seniors, their hoped-for life style after ending their working days is threatened. People are living longer than their parents did, so will collect Social Security benefits for many more years than what Congress expected and President Franklin D. Roosevelt signed into law seventy years ago. Consequently, the amount of payroll taxes collected will only pay three quarters of the benefits promised to today's workers who are having payroll taxes deducted from their pay checks.

For elderly people already collecting Social Security benefits or expecting to collect them soon, their payments are pretty well guaranteed. It's the young and middle age working people whose benefits are at risk. Just take a few moments to read the warning on your last Social Security Administration statement: "Your estimated benefits are based on current law, and Congress has made changes to the law in the past and can do so at any time," It's dead certain when Congress chooses to Change the Social Security system, newer seniors will be hit hard.

Not too many years ago elderly people could depend upon their adult children to help them survive, but nowadays it seems more and more of their children are stretched by having difficulty taking care of themselves and their own youngsters. No one should expect or depend on financial help from their adult children, and it's not realistic, after a person stops working, to expect Congress to take care of all his or her needs. It's everyone's responsibility to sacrifice and put money away for when they can work no more.

Seniors are not the only people losing sleep worrying about their survival. It's a troublesome concern for working single women with children; the cost of clothing, feeding, medical bills and day care puts them always in debt. They are left with little, if anything, to put away for retirement and if working, are often forced to opt out of their employer's 401(k) pension plan.

In an attempt to make up for the dwindling Social Security funds, President George W. Bush pushed his plan to divert money from individuals' Social Security benefits to within the stock market.

However, his plan never passed. The stressful task imposed on millions of people who knew little to nothing about investing in the stock market, but who would have to decide which funds taken from their benefits should be invested, made his plan very unpopular.

Unfamiliar word? Check the glossary at the end of this chapter.

Forecasting Your Retirement Needs

There's no way to forecast exactly how much money you need to save for your retirement. Nonetheless, columnist Sandra Block reported in USA Today that the average single working person who's earning around $3,050 per month is on track to replace 59 percent of their working income in retirement. That she maintained, "is nowhere near enough!" Could you make do on less than $1,800 per month? That's what 59 percent of $3,050 is! Would you cut the TV cable and dig out the grubby old "rabbit-ears" with it's analog to digital converter box? Which would you throw out: 'phone, internet, or cell? Will you travel less? You won't want to do that! After all, for 50 years you've been planning to travel and visit your children and grandchildren when you retire. No more eating out? But now you only do that twice a month with friends whose social relationship you'll need more than ever. It's clear you will need more than 59 percent of your working income when you retire.

"A person should plan on having 85 percent of a working income in retirement," wrote Ellyn McColgan, the president of Fidelity Brokerage. Well, that means a single person earning $3,050 per month should plan on having a monthly income of @$2,592 in retirement. When you consider the rent for a small apartment runs from $600 to $1000 per month, and a couple of visits to a doctor's office plus medication can cost several hundreds, McColgan's 85% minimum seems to be right on. However, in 2006 an average 65-year-old person only received a monthly Social Security benefit of $1,361; less than half of what McColgan says is needed.

One thing is for certain: Social Security, without a supplemental income, pushes you over the brink, below the poverty level. So, it's not only prudent to put money away to create a supplemental income, it's imperative!

Of course it's difficult to put anything aside for the future, especially when you are living from pay-day to pay-day where each new day costs more to live than yesterday.

In the years between 2000 and 20006, we suffered two of

the largest increases in costs compared to a generation ago, an increase of 83 percent in mortgage or rent and 108 percent on health care. And both costs are still rocketing towards the stratosphere.

Don't despair! It's possible to create a supplemental income. You do it by slowly squirreling away small amounts of money in a Treasure Chest. These accounts are not for wealthy people who can afford $1,000 to open an account with a large broker or for a working person who has a 401(k) qualified plan with matching funds; it is however an affordable plan for people with low or medium incomes and perfect for single mothers. For those people who do have a qualified salary deferral pension plan, learn how much money you will need in retirement (Appendix 1) and you may decide it judicious to put small amounts of money in a Treasure Chest.

In the next three chapters you will read how easy it was for three people to save successfully by investing small amounts of money and watching it grow. You will learn how easy it is to create and manage your own account in one hour of your time, once or twice a year, with just a notebook and pencil or with a computer spreadsheet, No need to pay a broker, financial advisor, grumpy old relative or busy friend.

It's not only financially rewarding, it provides you a wonderful feeling of independence.

Glossary

Broker: A brokerage account from which you can obtain financial advice, buy and sell stock. Most brokerages require a deposit of $1,000 to open an account.

Funds: A sum of money or stock that is convertible into money.

IRA, 401(k) and 403(b): These are all qualified salary deferral pension plans. An IRA is a personal plan; 401(k) plans are for employees of public corporations and the 403(b) are for employees of not-for-profit and none-profit corporations. Money is paid into these plans from earned income before taxes and taxes are paid on money withdrawn from these plans.

Matching Funds: Many companies no longer contribute to pension funds. They now establish 401(k) or similar qualified plans for their employees and encourage them to contribute by matching from 4% to 6% of an employee's contribution, depending upon years of service,

Opt out: Low pay employees who cannot afford to have the minimum amount of money deducted from their wages required to enroll in a 401(k) or 403(b) salary deferral plan, have the choice of not enrolling.

Payroll Taxes: The 7.65% of your gross pay that is automatically withdrawn for Social Security and Medicare taxes.

Private Accounts: A proposed plan to take money from the current guaranteed Social Security system and divert it into personal accounts within the stock market.

Social Security Benefits: The amount of money you receive each month when you retire. Benefits are based on total Social Security taxes paid and the age at which you retired,

Supplemental income: Money withdrawn from savings, dividends, annuities or other sources to fill the gap between your Social Security benefits and poverty.

Treasure Chest: This is a self-managed savings account in which you regularly purchase dividend-paying stock, reinvest the dividends and buy additional stock with the dividends, without paying brokerage fees. You can stop your dividends from being reinvested when you retire or at any time you choose; instead you can have them deposited directly into your bank checking account, thus providing you with a supplemental income.

Chapter 2

People and their Treasure Chests

Saving Cumulatively

In January 2008, I was awed listening to Helen Thayer, author, speaker and explorer, telling of her trek to the magnetic North Pole. An extremely difficult and dangerous adventure, she accomplished with Charlie, her dog and only companion. Mrs. Thayer ended her story by telling how she made a plan and stuck with it through adversity. She then advised her audience, "A goal without a plan is merely a dream."

As a striker for a high school soccer team, Claire's goal is to place the ball into the back of the opposing team's net and she plans to achieve it by dribbling the ball past their defenders, then giving it a mighty whack. Realistically she will score once in ten chances. As a high school soccer player, Claire may have had a goal of someday playing in the Women's Soccer College Cup, It was easy with my acrylic palette, to beam her up to that level; but for Claire to achieve it in reality her plan would be to study hard, be accepted by a college and develop the necessary skills to be selected for their team. Anything less and her plan to participate in a Women's Soccer College Cup game would remain a dream.

Often in life we intend to do something we know is important, but just can't figure out how to get started. It seems there is a wall between what we should do and forming a plan to achieve it. Sometimes, if we are fortunate, as it was for the two young men, in the following story, a person intercedes and gives us direction

As was the custom, the electronic store gave Christmas bonuses to its employees. So when Fred and Jeff, two teenage computer technicians, were called into their department manager's office, they were expecting a check. "Sorry. It's not as much as you deserve," Steve explained. "Since you've only been with the company a few months, top management only lets me give you $200; anyway, guys, thank you both for doing a good job! Enjoy your holiday and have a great new year."

The amount was exactly what the two techs were expecting. They had already been informed of the store's policy by longer time employees and had formed definite ideas on how they intended to spend their money. They thanked their manager and started to leave, but he called them back. "Just a minute guys, I have some advice. Sit down, this won't take long. You're not very busy anyway."

Steve was very fond of the two youngsters. They reminded him of himself when he was their age. He had not been aware of his monetary options then, and made many mistakes. Perhaps he could help his two employees move their careers forward. "You're both very young and you're talented technicians, but you need to start saving to go to college, maybe get a degree while working part-time. I'm sure you've planned how you're going to spend your bonuses, but instead, consider investing it in stock. Watch it grow. If you spend it now, in a month it will be gone and forgotten."

"I've no idea about investing in the stock market," answered Fred, a good looking young man who had planned to buy perfume for his latest girl friend. He continued, "I've heard, unless you are lucky, you'll lose all of it!"

Jeff felt differently. "It sounds like a good idea, Steve; I'm planning to go to community college in a couple of years. I have a few dollars in my mother's Credit Union savings, but that's all. Like Fred, I know hardly anything about investing."

Steve was pleased at least one of the youngsters was interested in his future, "Well, it's like swimming, Jeff. The best way of learning is to jump in!" He got up from his chair and sat on the edge of the desk. "You probably saw in last Sunday's Times *Sempra Energy* is planning to expand into green sources of energy. I figure that would be a perfect investment for you."

Both young men were keen conservationists and interested in new ways of creating energy, so Steve's suggestion dovetailed with their ideas. Jeff asked, "How do we go about investing, Steve?"

Fred broke into the conservation, "Do we have to buy shares from a broker?" How much do they charge?"

That both technicians were sounding mature was very gratifying. "Yes, you will have to buy shares from a broker. But if you'll agree to invest in *Sempra Energy*, I'll pay the fees."

Jeff had been feeling held back by his limited knowledge and wondered how he could afford to take more classes. Steve's plan might be a way to get started. "Sounds okay to me. I'll go for it!"

Fred, however, was still unsure about risking his bonus. "It seems a good idea, but I was planning to spend the money on a Christmas present. Besides how do we know we won't lose all our money?"

"Who's the present for, Fred?"

"It's for my girl friend!"

"One of many or so I've been told, Fred. I'm sure you can buy her a present from what you earn without using your bonus." Steve was becoming a little impatient with the young man's reluctance. "I'm so sure you won't lose your two hundred that if you're really concerned, I'll guarantee it."

"How can you do that, Steve?"

"If you keep the stock for five years and at the end of that time, it's worth less, I'll make up the two hundred. How does that sound?"

"Okay, Steve. I'll give it a shot."

The next day Steve introduced his two employees to an acquaintance at *Saturna Brokerage Services* where they discovered how easy it was to buy stock. Steve paid the $39 fee for

each of their transactions, and since he wanted the shares registered in the young men's names and for them to receive paper stock certificates, he paid each an additional five dollars.

Before they left, the broker informed the young men, "You've both purchased eight *Sempra Energy* at $25 per share. You should receive your certificates by mail in about three weeks."

It was one of those infrequent sunny days that occasionally surprise us during Northwest winters. On the way back to the store the three stopped at Chipoties and decided to sit on the patio. Steve asked, "How does it feel to own part of a power company?"

"Right," said Fred, in a morose tone. "About a quarter of a ten millionth part, I guess."

Jeff sounded more energized. "Great! So what happens now, Steve?"

"You will get your first dividend on the next dividend pay date."

"About how much will we get?" Asked Fred.

"Well, Fred, according to their web-site, Sempra Energy's dividend rate is twenty-five cents. Multiply that by the number of shares you own. That's what you'll get."

"So will someone send us checks for two bucks?"

"Not necessarily, Fred. You can request the company pay you by check or have your money deposited directly in a bank account. But, there's a quicker way of building your savings. Do you remember in school you were taught the difference between simple interest and compound interest?"

"Dimly, I was never any good at arithmetic!"

"I remember," said Jeff. "When you put money in a bank you get simple interest, but if you leave it in the bank, you get more interest."

"Almost, Jeff: Compound interest is when your latest interest is calculated on your deposited amount plus your accumulated previous interest. When you buy shares of stock you get dividends. Dividends and interest are the same thing, money the bank or company pays you for loaning them your money. You have a choice. You can choose to have the company deposit your dividend directly into your bank account where it should receive the bank's interest, or you can reinvest the dividend back into the company to buy a fraction of a share. In that way, your shares increases by a small amount each quarter. That's the cumulative and fastest method of creating wealth"

Cautious Fred, believing in the adage, "a bird in the hand is worth two in the bush," decided to have his dividends deposited directly into his bank's savings account where, each moth, he would receive a statement showing his money's growth. On the other hand, Jeff, who was affronted by his bank's one percent interest, chose to be adventurous and, hopeful of doing better, signed up for *Sempra Energy*'s Dividend ReInvestment Program (DRIP).

Fred and Jeff's first dividend payment date was January 16, and as Steve had explained to them, since the dividend rate was twenty-five cents, each young man's eight shares earned a two-dollar dividend.

The two dollars was deposited into Fred's savings account where it began accumulating 0.083% per month interest. Jeff's dividend purchased 0.11 of a share; he then owned 8.11 shares of *Sempra Energy* and would earn slightly more on the next dividend pay date.

If the two technicians had been hoping to make a large capital gain on January 16th, they would have been sadly disappointed. At the beginning of 2001, the price of *Sempra Energy* fell from $25 to $18.12.

That was a very large drop in a little over two weeks. Steve's advice to get into the stock market did not appear to be very good. None of the three could have known the market was about to fall in value until close to the end of 2002.

When Fred learned his investment had fallen in value, he was pleased Steve had guaranteed his money.

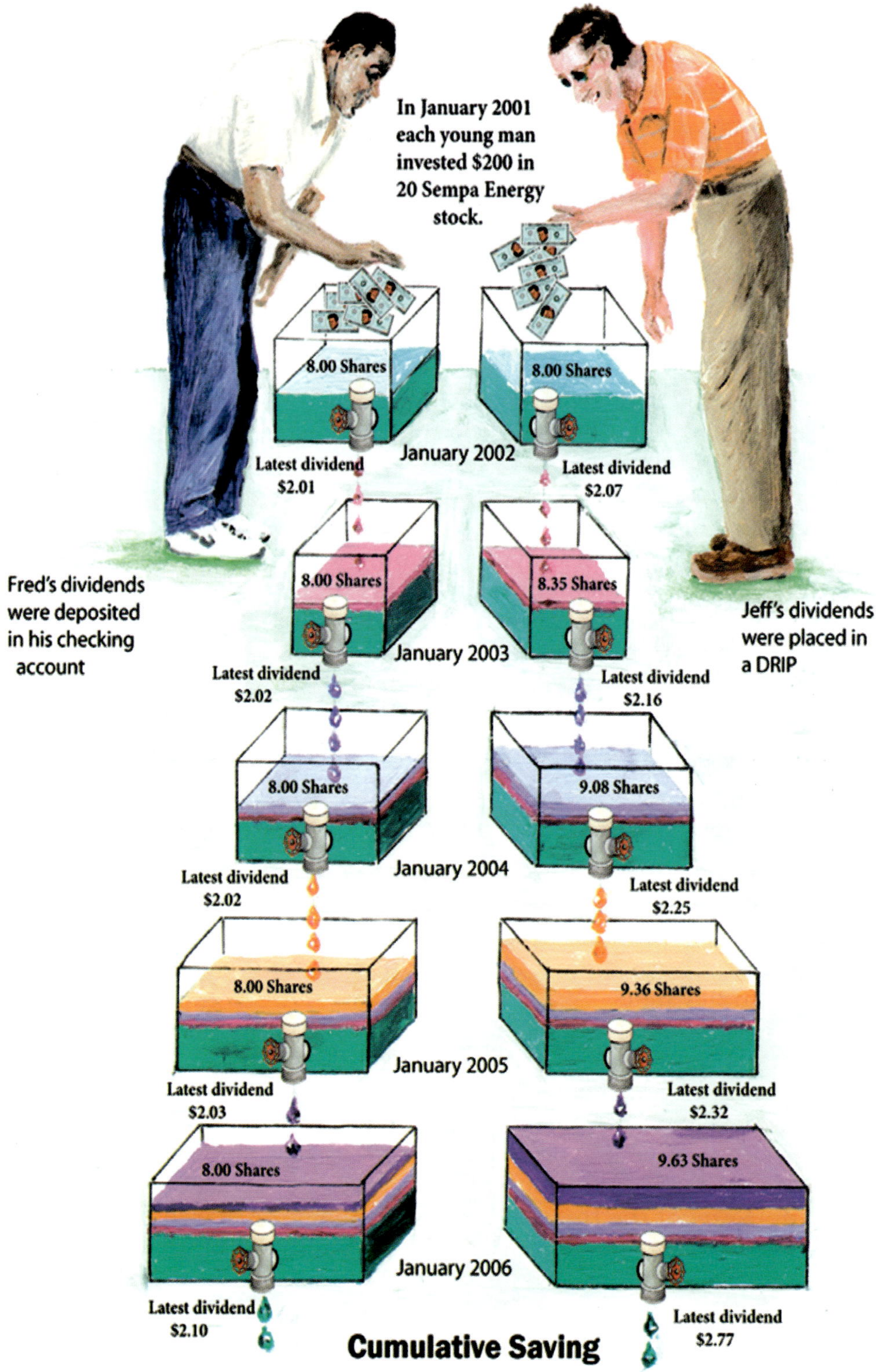

Cumulative Saving

Such a large fall in stock price is only disastrous if your retirement income is dependent on a capital gain. It's not so important when you are investing over the long haul, as you should be doing. It's an interesting fact, providing the dividend rate remains constant, when the stock price goes down, its

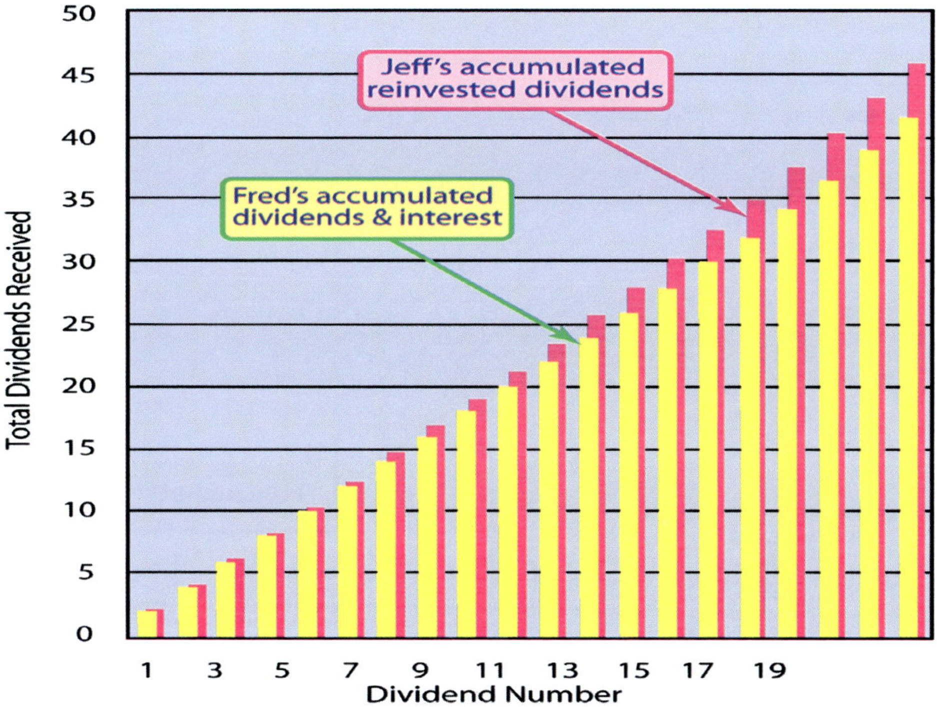

yield rises and visa versa. When Fed and Jeff made their initial investment, the stock price of *Sempra Energy* was $25 and the yield was (4 x 0.25/25.0) = 4.0%. It's an interesting fact, providing the dividend rate remains constant, when the stock price goes down, its yield rises and vica versa. As Jeff's stock fell from $25 to $18.12, its yield increased to (4 x 0.25/18.12) = 5.52% which resulted in more stock each quarter, and an increase future dividends.

Throughout the first ten months of wobbly stock prices when *Sempra Energy* was sometimes losing and sometimes gaining in value, the Board maintained its 25 cent dividend rate, so although Fred and Jeff were losing equity, they continued to receive their quarterly dividend. I first purchased shares of *Sempra Energy* in 1992 and immediately began reinvesting my dividends. At that date the company was called *San Diego Gas & Electric Co.*. By 1996, it had become the *Enova Corporation*, and then in 1998 changed its name once again to *Sempra Energy.*

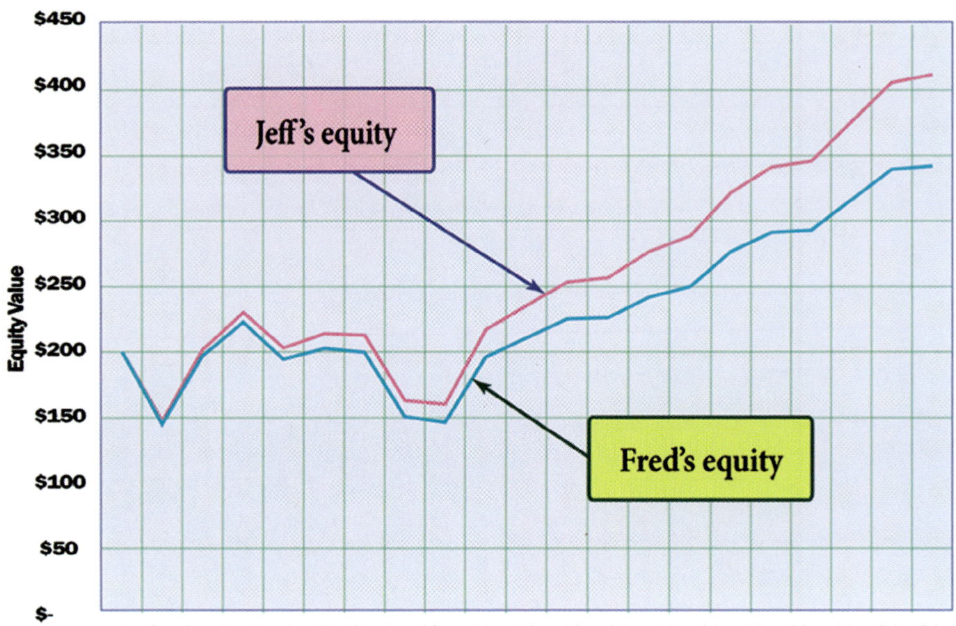

To ensure verifiable accurate records of the young men's investments over five years, I used the actual dates, stock prices and dividend rates from my *Sempra Energy* transactions.

Five years later, after dipping their toes in the stock market, Fred had received $42 in dividends and interest; due to the increase in Sempra Energy share price, his equity had grown to $384. When he subtracted his $200 initial investment, his gain was $184. Jeff did better. By reinvesting his dividends his stock gradually increased from 8 to 9.63. At the same time his equity curved up and away from Fred's at an increasingly steeper rate to produce equity of $412. Subtracting his $200 initial investment resulted in an overall gain of $212.

Saving Exponentially

Fred and Jeff demonstrated that it's possible to make money in the stock market by investing in dividend paying stock, and then doing nothing except sitting back and watching their money go to work. They both made reasonable gains. Fred, who had his dividends deposited directly into his bank's savings account, gained an average of 14.2% per year. Whereas Jeff, who reinvested his dividends, watched his account grow an average of 21,2% per year. Not only did the two young men make reasonable monetary gains, they also learned how to buy stock and a different way of savings.

It's not customary to make a single investment, such as Fred and Jeff did, and then let it remain untouched for five years. Most companies that provide DRIPs also include Optional Cash Payment (OCP) programs that allow people who are enrolled in their reinvestment plan to purchase additional shares or partial shares of stock directly from the company.

Buying stock involves some risk and you would be wise to be wary. Neither you nor anyone else can forecast a positive future of any company, its product, or its management. Like most people you've been told stories of men or women who invested in a "dead-cert-winner", only to learn later, to their regret, that the stock was in its death throes. Take heart; certainly there is some risk, but it's not as scary as you have been told.

Unless you can come up with a better way of creating a retirement income, open a DRIP now and save on a regular basis with an OCP. No matter how difficult it is for you to save, you can do it! Take time out, be quite, and think of where you can make a sacrifice. What can you do without? You can do it, just as Susan did!

"Hi, Ginny, how are you doing?" Susan asked another single mother she'd met at the farmer's market the previous Saturday.

"I'm doing fine, Susan, how about you?"

"Oh, I don't know. Stressed out I guess. Having to deal with Barbara's dad; he won't cough up the child support payments. I've just scanned six weeks Lotto, and of course, won nothing!"

For the past four years, Susan, an attractive, twenty-six-year-old working single mother has been in the habit each week of purchasing five dollars worth of quick-pick Lotto numbers. In the beginning, she was confident of winning and being rich for the rest of her life. On those days her newspaper printed the winning numbers, whatever the weather, Susan would grab a robe and race outside for the paper. Once back inside the apartment, she would check out the numbers before getting properly dressed.

Months later she realized the odds of winning Lotto's millions were stacked against her. Nevertheless, Susan continued to buy her five dollars worth of quick-pick chances, then, off-handedly consigned the receipts to the depth of her hand bag.

"That's tough," said Ginny. "Look, there's a booth open in Caffe Ladro's expresso bar. Let's grab it!" They both sat down, and then Ginny immediately stood to place an order. "Low-fat, sugar-free, latte, right?"

"That would be nice, thanks!"

When Ginny came back with the lattes, Susan said, "Thanks again, I really appreciate it. This makes my day."

"I'm glad to do it. Like me, you're probably having trouble paying bills. You on welfare?"

"Of course. After paying the rent and Barbara's child care, there's hardly anything left from the paltry amount they pay."

"Yet you still buy Lotto?"

"Yes, but only five quick-picks; I've got to win. It's the only way I'll survive."

"Susan, you know there's zero possibility of winning. When you waste $5 each week on Lotto, it means you're losing $260 ever year. In four years, that's more than $1,000 down the drain."

"I can't face being poor for the rest of my life. I've got to keep trying."

"I believed the same thing, but there's a better way, and it won't cost you any more. Let me tell you about DRIPs!"

"Oh, I know all about drips. I've dated a few and I'm hard up now because a drip won't pay the money he owes me."

"Not that kind of drip. I've dated a few of those myself; they're a common disease. But now I have a DRIP that pays

Beginning in January 1995, and for the next 12 years, Susan saved $5 every week. Each time her savings reached $50 she invested it in a Texaco DRIP.
In four years Susan had invested $1,000
December 1998 $1,312
Latest dividend $10.30
In eight years Susan had invested $2,000
December 2002 $2,869
Latest dividend $29.24
December 2006 $8,610
All 148 transactions are in Appendix 3.
In twelve years Susan had invested $3,000
Latest dividend $60.87
Exponential Saving

me regularly every three months. I'll tell you how to go about getting one for yourself."

That conversation occurred towards the end of 1994. After Ginny explained the advantages of a DRIP, Susan made a resolution to stop wasting her money on Lotto; instead she'd put her five bucks into a DRIP.

Starting on January 1, 1995, instead of buying Lotto numbers, Susan put her weekly five-dollar bill in a washed-out dog-food can, then continued to do so every week until she accumulated $50. During those ten weeks, she downloaded information about companies that permitted DRIPS, searching for one she believed would be safe. There were so many companies Susan had never heard of, she felt overwhelmed. However, for years she had carried a *Texaco* gasoline credit card in her wallet and believed that was proof her investment would be safe. Seeing on the *Texaco* web-site she could open a DRIP with as little as $50, clinched it. *Texaco Inc.*, would get her money. (That was in 1995. Ten years later there was no $50 *Texaco* DRIP and finding any company that allows you to open a DRIP with as little as $50 is hard to come by.

When Susan purchased her shares directly from *Texaco* she made a better deal than Steve. The $42 broker's fee that he paid would have purchased 1.76 more stock and his first dividend would have been $5.44 instead of $5.00, a gain of almost 10%.

Ten weeks later, on March 5th, after she had started saving, Susan made an application for a *Texaco Corporation* DRIP account and enclosed her check for $50. After two weeks had passed, Susan received a "Transaction Statement" in the mail that reported on March 17th she had bought 0.76 fraction of one *Texaco* share at a price of $65.55 per share.

Susan purchased shares in *Texaco*, but unlike buying Lotto numbers, she only lent her money to *Texaco*, Inc. She can always get it back any time she chooses, by selling her shares.

Although Susan was disappointed she owned less than one share, she persevered with her plan and sent her second $50 check, accompanied by a "Transaction Request Form", indicating the money was an "Optional Cash Payment."

On June 7th, she received an "Investor Service Plan" statement showing two cash payments of $50 and her first quarterly dividend of

$1.21. The amount was calculated by multiplying the 1.51 shares she held on her first Record Date by the 0.8 dividend rate. The reinvested $1.21 purchased a 0.02 fraction of a $68.04 share. Susan thus owned 1.53 shares.

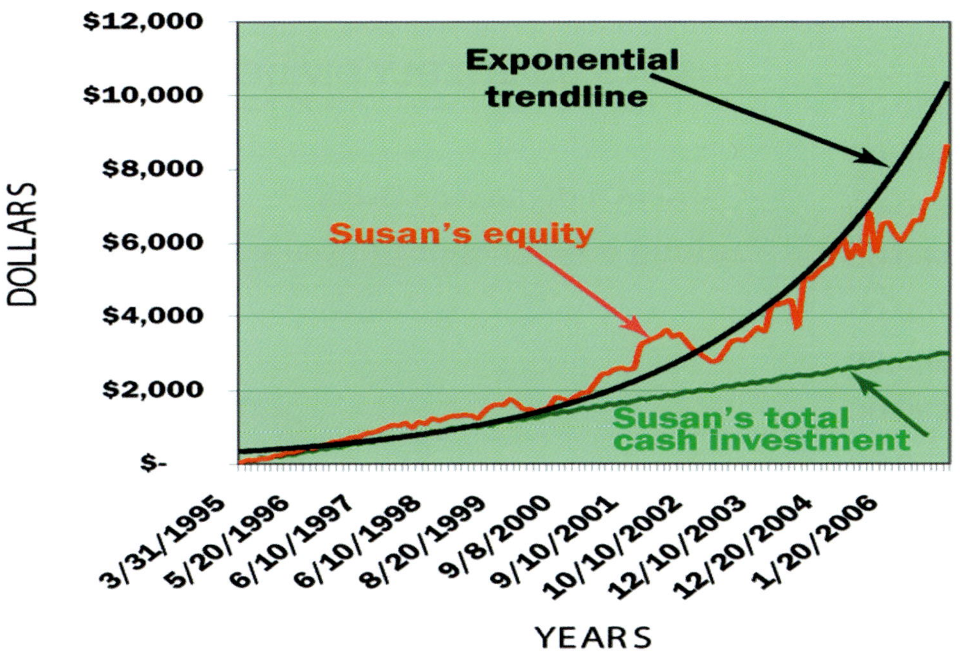

The year 2000 began with a sharp fall in the stock market. It was a period of anguish for most investors who could do nothing but cry, seeing their investments taking a nose dive. From its high point in December 1999, the market plunged down by 38% over two years.

As the price of Texaco shares fell, Susan saw her equity lose ground. Since she did not pay the 2% to 3% annual fees, as did those people who invested in mutual funds, 401(k)s, or other qualified retirement plans, her equity fell more slowly and recovered faster.

For Susan, the falling stock prices had a positive effect. As the *Texaco* shares fell and the company maintained its 25¢ dividend, the amount of shares she received each quarter increased, so although Susan's plan only gained $494 in value during the second four years, the number of her shares almost doubled, increasing from 23 to 42.

After putting away 71¢ each day for 12 years, Susan's DRIP accumulated 118 shares of *Texaco* stock, worth 48,610 and a quarterly dividend income of $60.88. That's not much, you might think, but ask any retiree who is relying solely on his or her Social Security payment if a $61,00 check every quarter would come in handy.

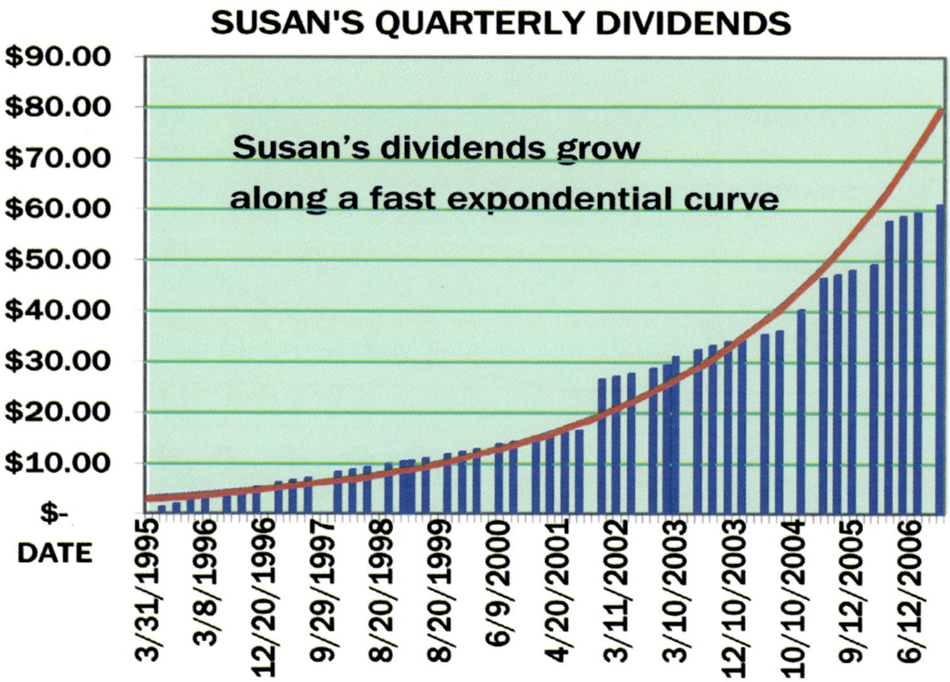

When you reinvest your quarterly dividends as Jeff did, your account grows cumulatively. However, when you regularly add cash to your account, as Susan did you create a second cumulative curve, The combination causes your account to grow at the fast exponential rate.

I began purchasing shares in *Texaco* in December, 1992 and immediately enrolled in their DRIP. I continued to reinvest my dividends and make occasional optional cash payments when it was acquired by the Chevron Corporation. The actual data from my DRIP account was used to provide accurate stock prices and dividend rates in Susan's Statements of Accounts, for 1995 through 2006 shown in Appendix 3, and beyond 2009 projection graph, Appendix 4.

Glossary

Broker: The person from whom you can buy or sell shares of stock.

Brokerage Account: An agency from which you can buy or sell shares of stock, you can arrange for your salary, retirement and Social Security benefits, interest and dividends to be paid directly into a brokerage account which will also be responsible for paying outstanding bills from the account.

Broker's fees: The costs involved in buying, registering, or selling stock. They may also include custodial fees, trust administration fees, and other expenses you paid for managing your investments.

Capital Gain: The cost basis of your capital assets including stocks, bonds, etc., minus the actual or potential gross sales price.

Compounding: You compound your money when you build wealth on top of freshly created wealth as well as on top of your initial investment. If you start with $100 and ear 4 1/2% in year one, you'll earn $4.50 and have $104.50. If you earn 4 1/2% in year two, you'll earn $4.70 and have $109.20.

Direct deposit: Some companies that pay dividends do not have reinvestment plans. They either send a check or transfer your dividend directly into your bank or credit union account.

Dividends: Dividends are distributions of money, stock, or other property paid to you by a corporation or company. Most distributions are paid in cash (by check). However, distributions can consist of more stock, stock rights, other property, or services.

Dividend Rate: The amount of the dividend paid per share per quarter.

Dividend ReInvestment Plans (DRIPs): These plans allow an investor to purchase shares of stock directly from a company and allow dividend payments to be reinvested in more stock.

Exponential: A fast increase expressed in terms of a designated power of e, the base of natural logarithm.

Optional Cash Payments (OCP): Voluntary cash purchases of additional shares in a DRIP.

Quarterly Dividend: These are cash dividends paid regularly on the quarterly record date. The amount is the product of the number of shares owned and the dividend rate.

Rate: Abbreviation of "the quarterly dividend rate."

Scanner: An electronic device that converts a digital bar code into alphanumerical data and sends it to a database.

Stocks: Investments that represent a share of ownership in a company. Stocks are traded on markets or exchanges where their prices can go up or down. Some stocks also pay dividends.

Stock Certificates: The certificate is proof of ownership of a specific number of shares. The name on the stock certificate refers to the shareholder of record.

Trendlines: Trendlines are also called regression analysis, are used to graphically display trends in data. You can use regression analysis, to extend a trendline predict future values.

Yield : The annual distribution of dividends paid on a share of stock divided by the market price of the stock.

Chapter 3

About Dividend Reinvestment Plans

Obviously your Social Security payments won't cut it; so what are your plans for creating a supplemental income? If you plan to grab the pot of gold from a leprechaun before the rainbow disappears, you'll need a back-up plan. If you seek the goose that lays golden eggs or plan on winning Lotto, you'll need a back-up. Whether you do or don't have a way to avoide standing in line at a food bank, it makes sense to learn about dividend reinvestment plans.

Not many people choose to read the financial section of their newspaper. However, should you do so, you've possibly read about CEOs of large corporations who earn in the millions and wondered how they make such lucrative salaries. Well, the successful ones keep their positions when, time after time, they make decisions that generate a profit for their companies; then, with advice from their Board of Directors, they figure out how their profits should be allocated so as to boost their investors' equity.

Of all the people who invest in public companies, the most important are the managers of large mutual funds. These people are responsible for increasing the wealth of their many clients; their clients' investments are maintained in very large numbers of shares of stock from a diverse range of companies.

Since such managers contol the investment of tens, or hundreds of thousands of shares, they are able to bring a great deal of pressure on

At least once each year, the CEO and the Board must decide how to allocate their company's profit by either increasing the cash dividends or by enhancing the company's assets. Should they choose to increase the shareholder's dividends, it gives the stock's yield a boost, thus making the stock more attractive. This immediately creates a demand for the shares and, hopefully, raises their market price. When the Board chooses to enhance the company's assets by expansion, research, development, purchasing new tools or equipment, or by acquisitions, they do so to ensure growth in future sales and profit.

The CEOs and Boards of Directors of more than one thousand large and small corporations figured they could make *both choices* by setting up Dividend Re-Investment Plans (DRIPs). Increasing the cash dividends pushes up the share's price and when those same cash dividends are reinvested back into the company, money is made available for enhancing the company's assets.

Now we have more than 1100 companies that offer DRIPs; programs which allow current shareholders to purchase stock directly from the company without the services or cost of a broker, and the dividends the shareholders receive are automatically reinvested by the company to buy more shares for the shareholder, thus increasing their investment in the company.

Optional Cash Payments

Most companies that offer DRIPS also allow you to buy additional shares directly from them. The rules governing their Optional Cash Payments (OCP) are published in their prospectuss, which also explains when, and how often, the company buys OCP shares; for example, Pfizer buys stock weekly, whereas Horizon Financial only buys stock on the quarterly dividend payment date. A permitted minimum and maxiimum amount of monthly and annual OCPs is included in the prospectus; the typical minimum is $50 for a single purchase and usually the maximum can not exceed $120,000 in one calendar year.

The Boards of more than a thosand companies did not set up DRIPs for anyone's benefit, other than their own; their objective was to increase the value of their company's stock and in so doing, keep their well-paying jobs! We live in the USA, a capitalist country. Its economy relies upon its entire people with incomes of all sizes who are willing to invest their money to provide tools, staff, training , and so forth. It's from such large, medium, and small capital investments that companies grow, an economy flurishes and jobs are created. It's up to us, you and me, people with low and medium incomes to also become capitalists. Go ahead! Take hold of the opportunity the Boards created. Invest cumulatively in their DRIP and do so without paying a broker to buy your shares or a Financial Advisor to manage your Treasure Chest.

Shareholder's Voting Responsibilities

The law insists, once you become a registered shareholder of a public operated company or corporation, you must be sent copies of the Corporation's annual financial statements, related management's discussions and analysis (MD&A) and that you receive an invitation tp special shareholders meetings. That is unless you inform the Corporation otherwise.

As a registered shareholder, you have the right and responsibility to vote (or assign a proxy,) or not to vote, for or against the selection of Directors, policy changes and financial auditors. You will also be asked by various conservation or civil rights groups to vote for proposals they've placed on the meeting's agenda.

By now, you should have a good idea about DRIPs, OCPs, and the stock market in general. You now know it's possible for you to save and have a supplemental income when you retire. However, it will only happen after you make the effort to enroll in a DRIP. So, step up! Now!

Glossary

Acquision: The act of acquiring another company.

Automatic Renvestment: Many Corporations pay a cash dividend four times a year to people who own stock in the Corporation. Usually the cash dividend is transferred as a direct deposit into the stock owner's bank account. However, many Corporations set up a plan that automatically uses the cash dividend to purchase additional stock and fractions of stock for the stock owner, thereby increasing the value of the stock owner's investment and the amount of future cash dividends.

Board: Means Board of Directors.

Board of Direcrtors: An organized body of administrators elected by the shareholders of the company to recruit and advise the CEO, and to appoint independent financial auditors.

Brokerage Account: An agency from which you can buy or sell shares of stock. You can also arrange for your salary, retirement and Social Security benefits, interest and dividends to be paid directly into a brokerage account which may also be responsible for paying outstanding bills from the account.

Broker's fees: The costs involved in buying, registering, or selling stock. They may also include custodial fees, trust administration fees, and other expenses you paid for managing your investments.

Capital Asset: Property you own for investment is a capital asset. Your capital asset is the number of shares you hold in the Company multiplied by the market price per share.

CEO: Chief Executive Officer of a Company or Corporation.

Equity: In this book, equity means your total number of shares in a company or corporation multiplied by the latest market price of the stock.

Mutual Funds: An investment company that offers and manages a portfolio of securities and shares of stock to a large group of investors.

Profit (Business): The difference between income and business expenses including salaries plus fringe benefits, transportatio, advertising, telephone, mail, replacemnt of goods and material taken from inventory, etc. And all taxes.

Profit (Investor): The capital gain, less the IRS 1040 Schedule D capital gain taxes (Currently 15%) plus other selling costs such as telephone calls and returning stock certificates by registered mail.

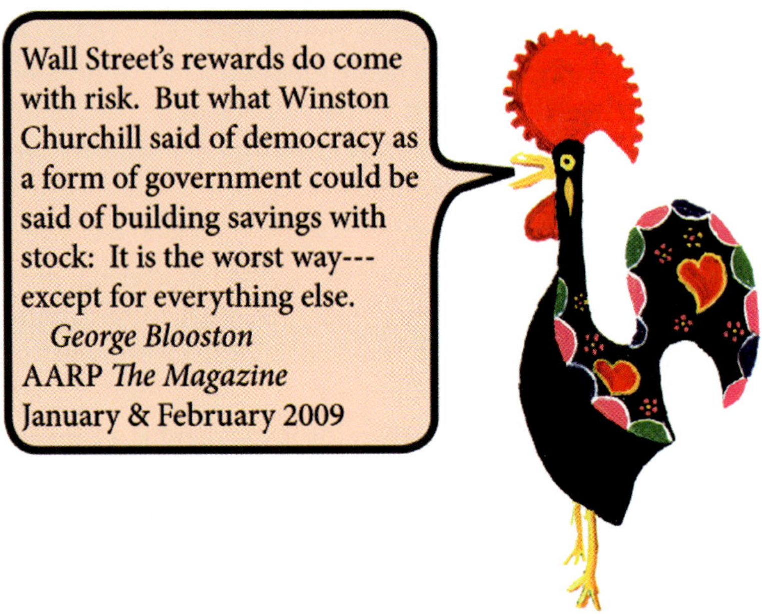

Chapter 4

Launching Your First DRIP

It's incredible how fast change occurs; fifty years ago, the invention of the transistor ended the industrial age and began the digital age which then made the present information age possible. Way back in that industrial age, business people tried to make a fortune by carting their goods to a merchant ship and sending them across the ocean for trade. They would then wait and pray their investment would survive storms, pirates and other scoundrels, to return safely with their fortune. It was in such a setting that mother pacified their hungry children by saying, "We'll have plenty when our ship comes home." Mothers no longer use such platitudes; their kids now hear, "We'll have everything, when I win Lotto." You and I know the chances of a mother or anybody winning Lotto is as likely as grandmother's fantasy ship coming home.

In this information age you don't have to cart your goods anywhere. The internet makes it easy to launch your investment in a DRIP, where it is safe from hurricanes, buccaneers or other villains.

Now you have read Parts 1 and 2, you are either eager to make up for lost time or are still procrastinating. Perhaps you have been warned by your family or acquaintance, against investing in a DRIP, warned by people who seem always to know of somebody who lost their shirt in the stock market. Perhaps you are still fearful of investing $250, or as little as $50, without a guarantee of gain, but with the possibility of losing. It's normal to be afraid of losing a few dollars and having to hear the "I told you so!" However, when you take reasonable precautions, there's a low probability you will lose; on the other hand, the probability of your being successful with your first DRIP, as Jeff and Susan were in Chapter 2, is extremely high. Success with your first DRIP will get you hooked; soon you'll be boasting of your stock market know-how to every cynical naysayer.

I discovered three methods of selecting a company from those 12,000 that offer DRIPs and will describe the two most suitable for your first venture. The first, which I call my short-cut method, quickly reduces your choice of a company to four or five. As a matter of fact, it was by using such means in 1994, I discovered SCEcorp (now Edison International) in The Los Angeles Times.

Read the Dividends and Yields table printed once or twice each week under Local Stocks or a similar title, in the business section of your newspaper. Highlight those companies with which you have an economic relationship; these are the natural gas, electric power, gasoline, banks, restaurants, and stores where you are a customer or do business. Your next step is to reduce the length of the list. Cross off those highlighted businesses that do not pay dividends; they are definitely unsuitable.

By now you've probably whittled your list to less than twenty; reduce it further by comparing the stock's percentage yields. If your newspaper does not publish yields, calculate them by multiplying their quarterly dividend rate by 400 and dividing the result by the stock's latest price.

Yield is a fuzzy number. It changes hourly as the stock price moves up or down, then changes again, but less often as the Board adjusts the dividend rate. To build your Treasure Chest and thereby create your retirement income, your investment needs a minimum yield greater than the current inflation rate, which at this time is around 1½%. However, as a novice investor you should be wary when you read of a stock that's producing a yield over 5.0%. Except for special cases, such as Real Estate Investment Trust Funds, a high yield raises the suspicion of something wrong with the company. It's safer to invest in companies that have a moderate yield, so delete any of your highlighted companies whose yield is less than 1½%, or more than 5%.

Your list should be down to a handful, so it's time to telephone the Investor Relations department of the remaining companies and ask if they offer a dividend reinvestment program. If they do, request a prospectus and an application package. If not, cross them off your list. Alternately, if you can access the internet from your home or at your public library, search for www,(company's name).com and link to *Investor Relations*, establish if they offer a DRIP, and download their prospectus and an application.

		52-WEEK				
COMPANY	DIV/YIELD	LOW	RANGE	HIGH	LAST	NET CHG
AMIS Hld	.../...	6.50		13.05	7.59	-.08
AVI Bio	.../...	2.19		4.17	2.41	+.08
AlskAir	.../...	21.15		44.52	24.57	-.76
Amazon	.../...	36.30		101.09	90.91	+.35
AmbassGp	0.46/2.6	16.80		41.08	17.99	-.35
AmEcol	0.60/2.7	17.26		24.50	22.24	...
AmWstBcp	0.16/.9	14.84		25.09	17.94	-.21
Avista	0.60/2.8	18.19		27.09	21.49	+.11
BannerCp	0.80f/2.7	27.63		45.87	29.23	-.73
BarrettB	0.32f/1.9	15.75		27.70	16.45	+.07
Bioject h	.../...	0.35		1.71	.43	+.02
Blount	.../...	10.61		14.36	11.74	-.53
BlueNile	.../...	33.22		106.16	72.44	-1.37
Boeing	1.40/1.5	84.60		107.83	91.79	-.75
Bsquare	.../...	2.41		7.48	6.21	+.02
Captaris	.../...	3.89		9.09	3.97	-.09
CardiacSci	.../...	7.40		11.50	8.30	-.13
CascadeBc	0.40f/2.3	16.36		31.90	17.04	-.30
CascdeCp	0.72/1.2	47.15		89.87	58.17	-2.16
CascadeFn	0.36f/2.6	13.01		18.25	14.11	+.45
CascadMc	.../...	8.21		14.63	9.28	-.17
CelebExp	1.25e/...	7.02		11.45	8.83	-.02
CellTher rs	.../...	2.38		7.80	2.61	+.02
CityBank s	0.60/2.9	19.63		36.45	20.90	+.10
Clearwire n	.../...	12.12		35.41	14.25	-1.32
Coeur	.../...	2.98		5.48	4.39	+.22
Coinstar	**.../...**	**25.40**		**34.97**	**25.31**	**-.82**
ColdwtrCrk	.../...	7.31		26.74	8.14	-.11
ColBcOR	0.40/2.3	16.46		27.05	17.40	+.06
ColBnkg	0.68/2.3	24.71		36.20	30.19	-.62
ColSprtw	0.64f/1.4	44.08		70.93	47.35	-.66

If you don't have any success with my short-cut method, you will have to resort to method number two. This will require you spend time carefully searching for a company that's highly rated and whose prospectus matches your needs. The means I use for that purpose is Charles B. Carlson's Drip Investor - Directory of Dividend Reinvestment Plans. If you decide to purchase a copy, (see page 29), make sure you obtain the latest version. This directory of over 11,000 companies offering DRIPs provides a profile of each company, a performance rating, and a recommendation of each plan as "attractive" or "unattractive."

The Prospectus

Once you have your list of promising companies, Carlson's directory provides telephone numbers where you can request a prospectus and a DRIP enrollment form. Since requirements, dividend rate, fees and so forth change at any time, it's important to obtain up-to-date prospectuses from each plan before making your final choice. Most companies publish their prospectus as a booklet which gives the requirements for participating in the company's plan, the address and telephone number of their transfer agent, and directions for making your initial investment.

Each year the number of companies that allow a Direct Purchase of initial shares increases. For example, you can now make your initial investment in shares of *Pfizer Inc.*, manufacturer of *Viagra, Zoloft, Lipitor* and other pharmaceuticals with $200. *Popular Inc,* a Puerto Rico bank, requires $100 and *Pinnacle West*, a provider of electric power to customers in Arizona requires only $50.

Other companies require new applicants to already be a shareholder of at least one stock before being allowed to enroll in their plan. If you have your mind set on a company that does not allow direct purchase, you will have to buy your initial stock through a broker. In this case, you need to look in your telephone yellow pages for a Discount Stock Broker. Such brokers only charge for buying or selling stocks, rather than a Full Service Broker who also gives investment advice and charges you for it.

Several companies, such as *Edison International*, *Pinnacle West*, *Horizon Financial*, *Pfizer* and *Popular Inc.*, pick up the tab for OCPs. Others charge a fee that is usually less than a dollar. However, *General Electric* charges $3.00 to process each OCP, so if you intend to only make small OCPs, less than $60, you need to include such OCP fees in your comparative DRIP evaluations.

Once you become a registered owner of stock, you own a tiny piece of the company, and as a stockholder you find yourself embroiled in the corporate world. Once each year you should receive a copy of the company's . This document is full of financial matters of little concern to you, who own such a small equity. However, there's usually a lot of interesting information about discoveries, inventions, new processes and so forth your company has made during the previous twelve months. When you are finished with an Annual Report, remove the cover and side it under plastic cover of its DRIP binder.

You will also be invited to attend the special and annual shareholders meetings where you can vote to seat the company's directors and the accountants who will audit the company's books. If you are unable to travel to the meeting, you can vote by mail or the internet through a proxy. You may also be solicited by organizations with social or conservation agendas to vote the number of shares you own for or against such resolutions.

Shares of stock represent real property that can be bought and sold, willed or inherited in a similar manner as other assets. In an emergency when you need a loan from a bank and you have a low credit number, you can request the company where you have a DRIP to send you paper stock certificates. You can then deposit the certificates at the bank as security on a loan. During the time the bank is holding your stock and you are paying off the loan you continue to receive and reinvest its dividends.

Any person can open a DRIP regardless of their age, gender or race. However, the IRS requires the person enrolled in a DRIP to have a legitimate Social Security number. The stock must also be registered in the "shareholder's" name, not in a "street" name or brokerage name. When you purchase stock through a discount broker, you may be asked to register your stock in the brokerage name. It is important that you do NOT allow that. You must insist that the stock be registered in your name and pay any extra (typically $3.00) fee to ensure you receive a paper stock certificate. If you are married, you should register the asset with both names as JT(joint tenants).

Glossary

Application package. This is your invitation to open a DRIP; at a minimum it will contain the plan's prospectus and an application to join. It may also include the last annual report or the most recent quarterly report.

Annual report. The annual report delivered to all shareholders includes financial statements, market conditions and investment strategies that significantly affect the company's performance.

Direct purchase. The purchase of stock shares directly from the issuing company without involving the services of a broker.

Directory. Up-to-date compilation of DRIP listings that provides addresses, phone numbers, performance ratings to guide the novice investor towards the best stocks.

Discount stock broker. These brokers provide little more than bare-bones, but efficient service. They do not usually provide investment advice, but will be glad to purchase or sell small quantities of stock for you. As such, their fees are much more reasonable.

Full service broker. These are the large well known brokers that usually requires you to open up an account by purchasing at least 100 shares. They will be glad to give you investment advice and manage your account for an annual fee based on its value.

Joint tenants. This form of registration permits both husband and wife to be named on the stock certificate. You should also consider registering as Joint Tenants with Rights of Survivorship. On the death of one, the surviving tenant acquires sole title to the shares

.**Market price.** The last reported purchase price of the stock on the market where it is bought and sold.

Paper stock certificates. The document that describes the name of the issuing certificate, the number of shares purchased, the date of the purchase and the name(s) of the purchaser.

Performance rating. This rating is provided by financial analyses or publications. If you use Chuck Carlson's DRIP Investor, you will see performance rating from a highest of four stars (****) to the lowest single star (*).

Percentage yield. Yield usually expressed as an annual percentage. To calculate the annual percentage, multiply four times the quarterly dividend rate by 100 and divide by the stock's latest market price.

Prospectus. This document describes how you can make an initial investment and how to reinvest all or a portion of your dividends.

Shareholder. The purchaser or purchasers who own the shares of stock.

Shares. The number of shares of stock owned on the dividend payout date.

Street name. This refers to the Full Service stock brokers on Wall Street, such as Merrill Lynch, J.P. Morgan and Ameritrade.

Transfer agent. A financial firm, such as Bank of America, that handles the plan's transactions and record keeping. They are the entities that you'll usually transact with when using direct investment plans.

Chapter 5

Managing Your Treasure Chest

Once you own stock in a public company, it needs to be managed. Because the company's stock is in your name and pays dividends, you are responsible for its management. Merely by choosing a company, buying shares and enrolling in its DRIP, you have already completed most of your management tasks. Now, all that remains is to keep a permanent record of every transaction and make sure you pay any State and Federal dividend income taxes that are due.

Transaction records, stock prices, yields, dividends received and cost basis for each of your DRIPS are best kept up to date in company specific Treasure Chest three-ring binders. As a novice investor, you will often refer to the company's Prospectus, so avoid losing it, remove the staples and place its pages behind transparent page protectors in the binder, or put the booklet in one of the binder's pockets.

If you purchased your stock through a broker, he or she will send you a BUY TRANSACTION CONFIRMATION which shows your brokerage account number, the number of shares you purchased, the company from whom you purchased the shares and the price per share. It will also show the TRADE AMOUNT, the broker's COMMISSION, any State taxes, fees, the net amount, the trade date, settlement date and transaction number. You will need this information when the stock is sold in order to validate its base price, so it must be kept safe. Place it in the company binder. Within a couple of weeks after you bought stock you should receive your paper stock certificates; check the number of shares and confirm they match the number on your BUY TRANSACTION CONFIRMATION.

When you buy shares directly from a company you do not receive paper stock certificates; your shares are held for you in a Book-entry account. Unlike mutual funds where the ownership of stock is shared by thousands in the fund, shares in a Book-entry account are like paper certificate shares registered in your name, yours alone. You are the beneficial owner and enjoy the same shareholder benefits as you would with certified paper shares. Companies do not offer paper certificates unless you request them.

Many companies allow participants in their DRIP to deposit their stock certificates in the company for safekeeping. This saves the worry about losing your shares through misplacement, theft or fire. Keeping your stock certificates in a bank's safe deposit box is an alternative method, but only if you can find a way of hiding the keys where they would not be misplaced or forgotten after months or years, but readily found when needed.

Statement of Account

One to eight weeks after returning a completed Authorization Form, you should receive a *Transaction* or *Statement of Account* from your chosen company. The document is a legal receipt for the number of shares you purchased, the registered names on the account, the date and the amount you paid. Check that everything is correct. If it is not, telephone the company or the transfer agent immediately.

Once each quarter, the companies in which you own a DRIP will send

PINNACLE WEST CAPITAL CORPORATION
INVESTORS ADVANTAGE PLAN

STATEMENT OF ACCOUNT

The Bank of New York, Administrator
P.O. Box 1958
Newark, NJ 07101-9774

01
SEQ# 012180

Answers to many questions and requests are available by visiting The Bank of New York's website at: http://stockbny.com or
Email at: Shareowners@bankofny.com

1-800-457-2983

012180 XBX85201

Troy H, McCook
30911 Bard Road
San Ysidro, CA 9173

Company Number	1852
Account Number	000056
Record Date	11/01/06
Payment Date	12/01/06

Next Anticipated Investment Date WEEKLY

IMPORTANT TAX DOCUMENT ATTACHED

CURRENT DIVIDEND PURCHASE INFORMATION

Plan Record Date Position							
Held By You In Certificate Form Or Direct Registration	Held By Plan Administrator	Total	Rate	Gross Dollars Paid	Service Fees	Tax Withheld	Net Dollars Reinvested
0	2.2367	2.2367	.5250	1.17	.00	.00	1.17

YEAR-TO-DATE TRANSACTIONS

Transaction Date	Transaction Description	Transaction Dollars	Price per Share	Transaction Shares	Total Shares Held By Administrator
	BALANCE FORWARD				.0000
08/10/06	INITIAL INVESTMENT	50.00	43.7550	1.1427	1.1427
09/28/06	OPTIONAL CASH	50.00	45.7050	1.0940	2.2367
12/01/06	PLAN DIVIDEND	1.17	49.3700	.0237	2.2604

IF YOU HAVE ANY QUESTIONS REGARDING YOUR ACCOUNT, PLEASE CALL OUR TOLL FREE NUMBER OR VISIT OUR WEBSITE.

THE ATTACHED TAX DOCUMENT SHOULD BE RETAINED FOR TAX PURPOSES.

YEAR-TO-DATE SUMMARY

GROSS DIVIDENDS	TAXES WITHHELD	CASH CONTRIBUTIONS	SERVICE FEES	TOTAL FUNDS INVESTED	ADDITIONAL INCOME	FAIR MARKET VALUE
1.17	.00	100.00	.00	101.17	.00	111.60

you a Statement of Account similar to that shown for *Pinnacle West*. This document will also show your account number, the transaction dates, dividend rate, total plan record shares, a description of the transaction, the transaction amount, price per share, the number and fraction of transaction shares and the total shares held by the administrator.

Over several years, you will accumulate more DRIPs, and every years they will send you *Statements of Accounts*, and it will save a lot of future grief and possible IRS problems if you maintain all records pertaining to buying and selling stock permanently.

It's a good policy to place each quarterly *Statement of Account* in its folder as soon as you receive it. Either in December or early in the New Year, you will receive a *Statement of Account* that shows every transaction made during the past year. Check the information on the year-end Statement is the same as that shown on the quarterly Statements; if it is, recycle the three quarterly statements.

When it's time to sell your shares, the year end *Statement of Accounts* should satisfy any IRS audit but after a couple of years, it will require hours of digging to determine the cost basis. It's easy to solve that problem by creating a *Permanent*

(Company) Permanent Record Sheet

Transaction date	Dividend rate	Dividend received	Optional cash	Commission and fees	Share price	Shares received	Total shares	Basis of investment	Equity

Record Sheet for each DRIP you own. All you need is a couple of sheets of 8½" x 11" lined paper, a ruler, pencil and eraser. The needed arithmetic is no more than balancing a check book.

1. On the top line write the company name followed by Record Sheet.
2. Draw a Line under the title, completely across the paper.
3. Starting from under the horizontal line, close to the left, draw nine equally spaced vertical lines, to the bottom of the page.
4. Beginning at the left side in the first column, using two

lines if necessary, write the following labels: Transaction Date, Dividend Rate, Dividend Received, Optional Cash, Commission & Fees, Share Price, Shares Received, Total Shares, Investment Basis and Equity.

5. Draw another horizontal line under the words you have just inserted.

You have now created a *Permanent Record Sheet* (PRS) template and since you will be using copies for recording information for your present and future DRIPS, erase the company name from the heading at the top of the sheet before making copies.

Copy the data into the PRS columns from your BUY TRANSACTION CONFIRMATION or from the company's *Statement of Account*. The Investment Basis is the only number not contained on a *Statement of Account* and you or someone else will need to calculate it eventually when the stock is sold.

The Investment Basis is the total amount of money spent to purchase your stock and should be updated each time a new line of data is entered in the PRS. On the first line the Investment Basis is the sum of the Optional Cash you paid for the shares plus any Commission or Fees. On subsequent lines the Investment Basis is obtained by adding the Dividends Received, Optional Cash, Commission and Fees to the Investment Basis on the previous line.

Thus on line one of the

Pinnacle West Capital Corporation PRS is $250 Optional Cash, and since no fees or commission was paid the Investment Basis is $250. On the second line the $3.45 reinvested dividend is added to the $250 Investment Basis on the first line to produce an updated Investment Basis of $253.45.

Your Investment Basis does not include any fees the company paid for you; they are part of their business expenses.

Your equity is obtained by multiplying the market price of the stock by the number of shares you own on that particular

Pinacle West Capital Corporation
Permanent Record Sheet

Transaction date	Dividend rate	Dividened received	Optional cash	Commission and fees	Share price	Shares received	Total shares	Basis of investment	Equity
08/10/06	0.5250	--	50.00	0.00	43.7550	1.1427	1.1427	50.00	50.00
09/28/06			50.00		45.7050	1.0940	2.2367	100.00	102.2283
12/01/06		1.17	--		49.3700	0.0237	2.2604	101.17	111.5959

date. The Equity column serves no purpose except to give you joy or a headache. When the amount in the Equity column is higher than the amount in the Investment Basis column you have made a gain, and vica-versa. It often happens that when you start a new DRIP you lose paper money as did Jeff and Susan. If you don't panic, stick with your plan, eventually you begin to see a gain in value.

Reporting Your Dividend Income

Regardless of whether you hold stock in your own name or it's held by a broker in a "street-name", and you received $10 or more in dividends, you are responsible for reporting your ordinary dividends on line 9a and qualified dividends on line 9b of IRS Form 1040.

Before March you should receive a Form 1099-DIV from the company or its agent, reporting ordinary and qualified dividends paid the previous year. Even if you don't receive a Form 1099-DIV, you must report all your taxable dividend income on Form 1040, Schedule B, Part II. This simply means adding the quarterly dividends for the year from the PRS.

Ordinary Dividends are reported On line 5, list each payer's name and the amount of ordinary dividends received. Enter on line 6 the total of the amounts listed on line 5, and attach the schedule B to your Form 1040. Do not attach your Form 1099-DIVs to your Form 1040, instead, file them in their appropriate company binder.

☐ CORRECTED (if checked)

PAYER'S name, street address, city, state, ZIP code, and telephone no. Alvin Bond Fund 100 Wiley Street, Suite 567 Fairview, KY 42221		1a Total ordinary dividends $ 1,565.00 1b Qualified dividends $ 875.00	OMB No. 1545-0110 2007 Form 1099-DIV	Dividends and Distributions
		2a Total capital gain distr. $ 737.00	2b Unrecap. Sec. 1250 gain $	Copy B For Recipient
PAYER'S federal identification number 23-1XXXXXX	RECIPIENT'S identification number 221-XX-XXXX			
RECIPIENT'S name Troy H. McCook		2c Section 1202 gain $	2d Collectibles (28%) gain $	This is important tax information and is being furnished to the Internal Revenue Service. If you are required to file a return, a negligence penalty or other sanction may be imposed on you if this income is taxable and the IRS determines that it has not been reported.
		3 Nondividend distributions $	**4 Federal income tax withheld** $	
Street address (including apt. no.) 30911 Bard Road			5 Investment expenses $	
City, state, and ZIP code Your City, State and Zip Code		6 Foreign tax paid $	7 Foreign country or U.S. possession	
Account number (see instructions)		8 Cash liquidation distributions $	9 Noncash liquidation distributions $	

Form **1099-DIV** (keep for your records) Department of the Treasury - Internal Revenue Service

Depending upon the current IRS tax laws, your qualified dividends may be subjected to a lower tax rate than what applies to your other income. You need to figure your lower tax by completing the Qualified Dividend and Capital Gain Tax Worksheet, printed in the latest IRS Form 1040 instructions.

Part II Ordinary Dividends	5 List name of payer			
(See instructions on back and the instructions for Form 1040A, or Form 1040, line 9a.)	PINNACLE WEST		1	37
Note. If you received a Form 1099-DIV or substitute statement from a brokerage firm, list the firm's name as the payer and enter the ordinary dividends shown on that form.	PEPSICO		154	19
	SEMPRA ENERGY	5	264	47
	6 Add the amounts on line 5. Enter the total here and on Form 1040A, or Form 1040, line 9a	6	420	03

Note. If line 6 is over $1,500, you must complete Part III.

Part III Foreign Accounts and Trusts	You must complete this part if you **(a)** had over $1,500 of taxable interest or ordinary dividends; **(b)** had a foreign account; or **(c)** received a distribution from, or were a grantor of, or a transferor to, a foreign trust.	Yes	No
(See instructions on back.)	**7a** At any time during 2009, did you have an interest in or a signature or other authority over a financial account in a foreign country, such as a bank account, securities account, or other financial account? See instructions on back for exceptions and filing requirements for Form TD F 90-22.1		NO
	b If "Yes," enter the name of the foreign country		
	8 During 2009, did you receive a distribution from, or were you the grantor of, or transferor to, a foreign trust? If "Yes," you may have to file Form 3520. See instructions on back		NO

For Paperwork Reduction Act Notice, see Form 1040A or 1040 instructions. Cat. No. 17146N **Schedule B (Form 1040A or 1040) 2009**

Schedule B, Part II

Selling Your Stock

When it comes time to sell all or part of your stock held in a DRIP, most companies will arrange to sell the stock for you, some will do so without charging any brokerage commission. In either case, when you sell stock you are responsible for reporting Capital Gains or Losses and you must complete and attach Schedule D to your Form 1040. The data from the Form 1099-B you received from the company or a broker when you sell stock must be entered in the Schedule D.

If you held the stock for one year or less, you should use Part I of Schedule D and use Part II for Stock you held more than one year. The method of completing the two parts is the same.

Enter the name of the company and number of shares that you sold in column (a), i.e., **105.5 sh. Molson Coors.**

Since you acquired your stock through optional cash payments or reinvested dividends at different times, you enter

SCHEDULE D (Form 1040)
Department of the Treasury Internal Revenue Service (10)

Capital Gains and Losses

► Attach to Form 1040 or Form 1040NR. ► See Instructions for Schedule D (Form 1040).
► Use Schedule D-1 to list additional transactions for lines 1 and 8.

OMB No. 1545-0074
2008
Attachment Sequence No. 12

Name(s) shown on return: Troy H. McCook
Your social security number: 221 XX XXX

Part I — Short-Term Capital Gains and Losses—Assets Held One Year or Less

	(a) Description of property (Example: 100 sh. XYZ Co.)	(b) Date acquired (Mo., day, yr.)	(c) Date sold (Mo., day, yr.)	(d) Sales price (see page D-7 of the instructions)	(e) Cost or other basis (see page D-7 of the instructions)	(f) Gain or (loss) Subtract (e) from (d)
1						

2	Enter your short-term totals, if any, from Schedule D-1, line 2	2	
3	**Total short-term sales price amounts.** Add lines 1 and 2 in column (d)	3	
4	Short-term gain from Form 6252 and short-term gain or (loss) from Forms 4684, 6781, and 8824	4	
5	Net short-term gain or (loss) from partnerships, S corporations, estates, and trusts from Schedule(s) K-1	5	
6	Short-term capital loss carryover. Enter the amount, if any, from line 8 of your **Capital Loss Carryover Worksheet** on page D-7 of the instructions	6	( )
7	**Net short-term capital gain or (loss).** Combine lines 1 through 6 in column (f)	7	

Part II — Long-Term Capital Gains and Losses—Assets Held More Than One Year

	(a) Description of property (Example: 100 sh. XYZ Co.)	(b) Date acquired (Mo., day, yr.)	(c) Date sold (Mo., day, yr.)	(d) Sales price (see page D-7 of the instructions)	(e) Cost or other basis (see page D-7 of the instructions)	(f) Gain or (loss) Subtract (e) from (d)
8	17 Sh. Pepsicola	various	03.30.08	1,079 00	374 00	705 00
	0.2934 Sh. PacificCorp	various	09.28.08	11 00	6 00	5 00

9	Enter your long-term totals, if any, from Schedule D-1, line 9	9	0 00	0 00
10	**Total long-term sales price amounts.** Add lines 8 and 9 in column (d)	10	1,090 00	
11	Gain from Form 4797, Part I; long-term gain from Forms 2439 and 6252; and long-term gain or (loss) from Forms 4684, 6781, and 8824	11		0 00
12	Net long-term gain or (loss) from partnerships, S corporations, estates, and trusts from Schedule(s) K-1	12		0 00
13	Capital gain distributions. See page D-2 of the instructions	13		0 00
14	Long-term capital loss carryover. Enter the amount, if any, from line 13 of your **Capital Loss Carryover Worksheet** on page D-7 of the instructions	14		(0 00)
15	**Net long-term capital gain or (loss).** Combine lines 8 through 14 in column (f). Then go to Part III on the back	15		710 00

the date acquired as "VARIOUS," in column (b).

Enter the Date of Sale shown on the 1099-B in column (c) of Schedule D.

Unless the 1099-B indicates otherwise, the Total Sales Price shown is the gross sales price; enter it in column (d). If you sold all your stock in the company, enter the latest "Cost Basis" from its PRS in column (e). Subtract the amount in column (e) from the amount in (d) and enter the remainder in column (f). If the amount in (f) is a negative number, place it in brackets, i.e., (35). Add the amounts in column (d) and enter the total in Line 10.

Enter the total of the amounts in column (f) in Line 9, Line 15 and Part III, Line 16. If Line 16 is a gain, enter the amount on Form 1040, Line 13. However, if Line 16 is a loss, enter the smaller of the loss or $3,000, but if you are married and filing separately, enter $1,500.

Selling Fractional Shares

Sometimes a company is acquired by another, as *Scottish Power* did in year 2,000, when it acquired *PacificCorp*. At that time I had 124.2934 shares in *PacificCorp.*, DRIP of which 124 were exchanged for 72 shares of *Scottish Power* and a $10.84 check for the 0.2934 fractional shares.

I entered 0.2934 Sh. PacificCorp in column (a) of Schedule D, Various in (b), Sale price of $10.84 in (d). At the time of the acquisition, my Cost Basis in *PacificCorp.*, was $2,376, so the base cost of an average *PacificCorp* share was $2,376/124 = $19.16. Thus the basis of the 0.2934 fraction was ($19.16 multiplied by 0.2934) $5.62, which I entered as the column (e).

If you are not at ease in completing your tax returns, make an appointment and take your Forms 1099-DIV, 1099-B and "Cost Basis" amount from the companies Permanent Record Sheets to a free tax aide.

Glossary

Broker's commission. The fees a broker charges to purchase or sell shares of stock.

Buy transaction confirmation. The document that lists the date, name of stock, the amount of stock, the price per share, the buyer's name and tax number.

Book-entry account. An electronic record keeping system known as Direct Registration System (DRS) to track the number of shares held by each shareholder.

Cost basis. The total amount of money paid for a specific stock that includes all cash payments, all reinvested dividends and fees.

Capital gain/loss. You figure gain or loss on the sale or trade of property. The gain is the difference between the amount you realized from the sale or trade and the adjusted basis of the property. If the adjusted basis of the property you transfer is more than the amount you realize, the difference is a loss.

DRIP binder. Usually a ½" or 1" plastic binder that holds all the paper documents relating to a specific company's DRIP.

Ordinary dividends. These are the most common type of distribution from a corporation or public company. They are paid out of the earnings and profits of a corporation and are ordinary income to you. This means they are not capital gains. Ordinary dividends received will be shown in box 1a of the Form 1099-DIV you receive.

Permanent record sheet. It's good management to maintain a permanent record for each company in separate binders and to keep an updated cost basis for each investment.

Qualified dividends. These are ordinary dividends that under the 2008/09 tax law are subjected to the same 5% or 15% maximum tax rate that applies to net capital gain. They are shown in box 1b of the Form 1099-DIV you receive. Currently, qualified dividends are subjected to the 15% rate if the regular tax rate that would apply is 25% or higher, providing you meet the holding period. Qualified dividends are subjected to the 5% rate if the regular tax rate that would apply is lower than 25%, providing you meet the holding period; if you still own stock you have met the holding period but if it has been sold you need to get help with your taxes.

Chapter 6

Filling Your Diverse Portfolio

No matter where you invest what's left of your paycheck, after forking out your earnings for essentials, your investment carries some risk. Be it a family restaurant, real estate, a small business or the stock market, each entails risk. Because you have invested in a *Treasure Chest* you need to protect it. The method investment companies use to reduce risk is by divesting their funds, spreading the risk by dividing their investments in a portfolio of companies. Most likely, money from your earnings that goes into an IRA, 401(k), 403(b) or other qualified salary deferral pension plans will be invested in thousands of companies. You have some small control over the diversification of your pension plans by choosing in which funds your deductions are placed, but little control over the choice of the companies in the fund.

However when you reduce the risk to your *Treasure Chest* by adding more DRIPs to your portfolio, you choose those companies that meet your requirements from the more than 1,000 that offer DRIPs. When you add additional DRIPs or optional cash payments to diversify your *Treasure Chest*, you choose a mix from companies that are unrelated such as power, pharmaceutical, retail, industrial, food and beverage, entertainment or banking. You can also diversify within a specific business area such as the power section: oil, fuels or wind-power.

The manager of your employer's qualified salary deferral pension plan chooses a diverse mixture of companies in which to place your money. He or she tries to choose a percentage of stock that promises high gain, but may have some risk and a percentage of stocks that have moderate or low growth, but are relatively safe. These stocks are gathered in a specific named fund in which the various percentages are assembled in a "target mix." Over time, the value of the stocks change significantly and thus the percentages also change. When the percentages of specific stocks or group of stocks moves outside of its allocated range it is referred to as "straying." Most commercial funds use a rebalancing method to identify and correct an investment when it strays from its target mix. This method involves selling and buying shares until the target mix is corrected. However, each action of buying or selling costs the owner of the pension plan money.

DRIPs are for people who want to invest consistently over the long term so rebalancing does not take place in a Treasure Chest portfolio by selling advancing and buying lagging stock, instead it is achieved by increasing the optional cash payments to those companies that are falling below your target mix.

Portfolio Tracking Workbook

As soon as you have more than a single DRIP, it's worthwhile to track and compare the results between your investments with a Portfolio Tracking Workbook (PTW). Such a workbook is an important tool; it allows you to readily identify and correct an investment when it strays from its target mix. All you need is paper, pencil and ruler to copy the 2009 Portfolio Tracking Workbook template shown on page 53.

A	B	C	D	E	F	G	H	I	J	K
Name	Qty.	Rate	Price	Basis	Dividend 1/4/7/10	Dividend 2/5/8/11	Dividend 3/6/9/12	Yield	2009 Dividends	Value
									$ -	$ -
Totals				$ -	$ -	$ -	$ -		$ -	$ -

Portfolio Tracking Workbook Template

Enter the company names in column (A). Copy the data in (B), (C), (D) and (E) from your latest Permanent Record Sheet. Multiply your quantity of shares in B by the rate in C, and place the result in whichever of the columns F, G, or H that lists the months the company pays dividends. Calculate the percentage yield in column (I) by multiplying the rate shown in (C) by 400 and dividing the result by the share price in (D). Multiply the dividends in (F), (H), or (H) by 4 and enter the result in J. Multiply the quantity of shares in (B) by their price in (D) and enter their value in (K).

Although Susan in Chapter 2 did OK with a single company, it was not an advisable plan. She could have reduced her chances of loss by spreading her $3,000 over three unrelated DRIPs and at the same time chosen companies which paid dividends on different quarters. By doing so, she could have received a dividend income monthly.

It would have been a good idea, for instance, to diversify by including Pfizer Inc., a pharmaceutical, and Popular, Inc., a banking company, in her portfolio. If she had done so, by the end of 2006, her Portfolio Tracking Worksheet would look somewhat like that shown below.

A	B	C	D	E	F	G	H	I	J	K
Name	Qty.	Rate	Price	Basis	Dividend 1/4/7/10	Dividend 2/5/8/11	Dividend 3/6/9/12	Yield	2009 Dividends	Value
Chevron	17.28	0.52	$80.20	$1,386	$8.99			2.6%	$35.95	$1,386
Pfizer	31.00	0.29	$24.15	$749		$8.99		4.8%	$35.95	$749
Popular	56.17	0.16	$15.40	$865			$8.99	4.2%	$35.95	$865
Totals	104			$2,999	$8.99	$8.99	$8.99	3.6%	$107.85	$2,999

A Diversified Portfolio Tracking Workbook

Glossary

Diversity. We don't know which stocks will be the winners and which will be the losers, so we create diversity by owning a variety.

Portfolio. An itemized list of investments, securities and commercial paper owned by an investor.

Portfolio tracking workbook. A table that can be used to show comparative data between the results of DRIPs in your portfolio.

Rebalancing. A method used by financial companies to return a group of investments back to their original target mix. Usually by buying and selling shares.

Stray investment. The purpose of an Aggressive Fund is to quickly increase its value. If after several months it has been successful, its value would have increased significantly in comparison to other stocks in its group and thus will have "strayed" from the original mix.

Target mix. Usually when you invest in a Mutual Fund, an IRA, 401(k) or 403(b), your total invested equity is split between various funds in a Target mix; for example 20% Aggressive Fund, 60% Moderate Fund and 20% Conservative Fund.

Wealth. The material or market value of something.

Appendix 1

Qualified Retirement Saving Plans

This page gives you a model for calculating the equity needed to create a minimum supplemental retirement income.

Some fortunate workers have been able to save by placing part of their pre-tax earnings into an IRA, 401(k), or 403(b) plan to provide a monthly distribution (supplemental income) from their funds after their retirement. For a $3,050 per month working person, in 2007 (page 5, Ellyn McColgan), the monthly distribution would have to be $1,231, the difference between a needed $2,592 and a Social Security benefit of $1,361.

To receive a $1,231 monthly distribution for 30 years from a savings plan that maintains its value after inflation, the distribution, plus management fees, must be less than the plan's monthly gain in value. Historically, that amount is around 0.004% (4.8% annual), which means the value of the savings plan must be maintained at $1,231/0.004 = $307,750.

The ($1,231/month) $14,772 annual distribution would be from pre-tax earnings and is subjected to Federal and State income taxes. However, the standard deduction for a single person (2008 IRS Form 1040) is $6,500 and the personal exemption is $3,500, the person only has to pay $478 taxes on a $4,772 taxable income. Since his or her adjustable gross income is $14,772, plus $8,166, which is half of the Social Security benefits, a total of $22,938 and less than $25,000; none of their benefits are taxable.

You can use the above example to calculate how large an equity your qualified salary deferral pension plan neeeds to be for you, your surviving spouse or partner after you are retired and alone. And, if you don't have a retirement plan you can use the same requirement for a $1,231 monthly dividend from your *Treasure Chest* retirement fund.

Appendix 2

Fred and Jeff's Cumulative Data

Fred's Account *Jeff's Account*

Date	Price	Rate	Total dividend & interest	Total shares	Value	Total dividend reinvested	Shares received	Total shares	Value
1/1/01	$ 25.00	0.25		8.00	$ 200			8.00	$ 200
1/16/01	$ 18.12	0.25	$ 2.00	8.00	$ 147	$ 2.00	0.11	8.11	$ 147
4/16/01	$ 24.61	0.25	$ 4.00	8.00	$ 201	$ 4.03	0.16	8.27	$ 204
7/16/01	$ 27.83	0.25	$ 6.01	8.00	$ 229	$ 6.10	0.22	8.49	$ 236
10/15/01	$ 24.31	0.25	$ 8.03	8.00	$ 202	$ 8.22	0.34	8.83	$ 215
1/15/02	$ 25.35	0.25	$ 10.05	8.00	$ 213	$ 10.43	0.41	9.24	$ 234
4/15/02	$ 24.97	0.25	$ 12.07	8.00	$ 212	$ 12.74	0.51	9.75	$ 243
7/15/02	$ 18.84	0.25	$ 14.10	8.00	$ 165	$ 15.18	0.81	10.56	$ 199
10/15/02	$ 18.29	0.25	$ 16.14	8.00	$ 162	$ 17.82	0.97	11.53	$ 211
1/15/03	$ 24.53	0.25	$ 18.18	8.00	$ 214	$ 20.70	0.84	12.38	$ 304
4/15/03	$ 26.23	0.25	$ 20.22	8.00	$ 230	$ 23.79	0.91	13.28	$ 348
7/15/03	$ 28.13	0.25	$ 22.27	8.00	$ 247	$ 27.11	0.96	14.25	$ 401
10/15/03	$ 28.28	0.25	$ 24.33	8.00	$ 251	$ 30.68	1.08	15.33	$ 434
1/15/04	$ 30.22	0.25	$ 26.39	8.00	$ 268	$ 34.51	1.14	16.47	$ 498
4/15/04	$ 31.26	0.25	$ 28.46	8.00	$ 278	$ 38.63	1.24	17.71	$ 554
7/15/04	$ 34.60	0.25	$ 30.53	8.00	$ 307	$ 43.05	1.24	18.95	$ 656
10/15/04	$ 36.43	0.25	$ 32.60	8.00	$ 324	$ 47.79	1.31	20.27	$ 738
1/18/05	$ 36.65	0.29	$ 35.00	8.00	$ 328	$ 53.67	1.46	21.73	$ 796
4/15/05	$ 39.62	0.29	$ 37.41	8.00	$ 354	$ 59.97	1.51	23.24	$ 921
7/15/05	$ 42.43	0.29	$ 39.83	8.00	$ 379	$ 66.71	1.57	24.82	$ 1,053
10/17/05	$ 42.76	0.29	$ 42.24	8.00	$ 384	$ 73.91	1.73	26.55	$ 1,135
Totals									
Ending	Equity		$ 384.36			1,135.19			
Capital	Gain		$ 184.36			935.19			
Percent	Gain		92%			468%			

Appendix 3.

Susan's 1995, 1996 & 1997 Statement of Accounts

Date	Action	Rate	Div's	Cash	Price	Shares	Total	Basis	Equity
3/31/1995	Cash	0.80		$ 50	$ 65.55	0.76	0.76	$ 50	$ 50
5/20/1995	Cash			$ 50	$ 66.90	0.75	1.51	$ 100	$ 101
6/9/1995	Div's	0.80	$ 1.21		$ 68.04	0.02	1.53	$ 101	$ 104
8/20/1995	Cash			$ 50	$ 64.30	0.78	2.31	$ 151	$ 148
9/8/1995	Div's	0.80	$ 1.84		$ 65.54	0.03	2.33	$ 153	$ 153
10/20/1995	Cash			$ 50	$ 71.65	0.70	3.03	$ 203	$ 217
12/8/1995	Div's	0.80	$ 2.43		$ 77.78	0.03	3.06	$ 205	$ 238
12/20/1995	Cash			$ 50	$ 80.02	0.62	3.69	$ 255	$ 295
3/8/1996	Div's	0.85	$ 3.13		$ 83.10	0.04	3.73	$ 259	$ 310
3/8/1996	Cash			$ 50	$ 83.10	0.60	4.33	$ 309	$ 360
5/20/1996	Cash			$ 50	$ 86.05	0.58	4.91	$ 359	$ 422
6/10/1996	Div's	0.85	$ 4.17		$ 83.23	0.05	4.96	$ 363	$ 413
7/20/1996	Cash			$ 50	$ 88.02	0.57	5.53	$ 413	$ 486
9/10/1996	Div's	0.85	$ 4.70		$ 92.80	0.05	5.58	$ 417	$ 518
10/10/1996	Cash			$ 50	$ 96.80	0.52	6.09	$ 467	$ 590
12/10/1996	Div's	0.85	$ 5.18		$ 99.58	0.05	6.15	$ 473	$ 612
12/20/1996	Cash			$ 50	$ 101.03	0.49	6.64	$ 523	$ 671
2/28/1997	Cash			$ 50	$ 102.49	0.49	7.13	$ 573	$ 731
3/10/1997	Div's	0.85	$ 6.06		$ 103.94	0.06	7.19	$ 579	$ 747
4/20/1997	Cash			$ 50	$ 107.50	0.47	7.65	$ 629	$ 823
6/10/1997	Div's	0.85	$ 6.50		$ 111.60	0.06	7.71	$ 635	$ 860
7/10/1997	Cash			$ 50	$ 112.80	0.44	8.15	$ 685	$ 920
9/10/1997	Div's	0.85	$ 6.93		$ 120.71	0.06	8.21	$ 692	$ 991
9/10/1996	Cash			$ 50	$ 120.71	0.41	8.62	$ 742	$ 1,041
9/29/1997	Div's	Stock Split			$ 60.35	8.62	17.25	$ 742	$ 1,041
11/20/1997	Cash			$ 50	$ 61.32	0.82	18.06	$ 792	$ 1,108
12/10/1997	Div's	0.45	$ 8.13		$ 54.51	0.15	18.21	$ 800	$ 993
	TOTALS		$ 42.2	$ 750					

Susan's 1998, 1999 & 2000 Statement of Accounts

Date	Action	Rate	Div's	Cash	Price	Shares	Total	Basis	Equity
1/20/1998	Cash			$ 50	$ 59.00	0.85	19.07	$ 850	$ 1,125
3/10/1998	Div's	0.45	$ 8.6		$ 57.42	0.15	19.22	$ 859	$ 1,104
4/9/1998	Cash			$ 50	$ 61.04	0.82	20.04	$ 909	$ 1,223
6/10/1998	Div's	0.45	$ 9.0		$ 58.93	0.15	20.19	$ 918	$ 1,190
6/10/1998	Cash			$ 50	$ 58.93	0.85	21.04	$ 968	$ 1,240
8/20/1998	Cash			$ 50	$ 59.15	0.85	21.89	$ 1,018	$ 1,295
9/10/1998	Div's	0.45	$ 9.8		$ 59.40	0.17	22.05	$ 1,027	$ 1,310
10/20/1998	Cash			$ 50	$ 58.11	0.86	22.91	$ 1,077	$ 1,331
12/10/1998	Div's	0.45	$ 10.3		$ 56.82	0.18	23.09	$ 1,088	$ 1,312
3/101999	Div's	0.45	$ 10.4		$ 53.77	0.19	23.27	$ 1,098	$ 1,251
3/10/1999	Cash			$ 50	$ 58.85	0.85	24.12	$ 1,148	$ 1,420
6/10/1999	Div's	0.45	$ 10.9		$ 63.88	0.17	24.29	$ 1,159	$ 1,552
6/10/1999	Cash			$ 50	$ 63.88	0.78	25.08	$ 1,209	$ 1,602
8/20/1999	Cash			$ 50	$ 62.41	0.80	25.88	$ 1,259	$ 1,615
9/10/1999	Div's	0.45	$ 11.6		$ 67.25	0.17	26.05	$ 1,271	$ 1,752
10/20/1999	Cash			$ 50	$ 61.12	0.82	26.87	$ 1,321	$ 1,642
12/10/1999	Div's	0.45	$ 12.1		$ 55.49	0.22	27.09	$ 1,333	$ 1,503
12/20/1999	Cash			$ 50	$ 52.50	0.95	28.04	$ 1,383	$ 1,472
3/10/2000	Div's	0.45	$ 12.6		$ 50.48	0.25	28.29	$ 1,396	$ 1,428
3/10/2000	Cash			$ 50	$ 50.48	0.99	29.28	$ 1,446	$ 1,478
5/20/2000	Cash			$ 50	$ 51.48	0.97	30.25	$ 1,496	$ 1,557
6/9/2000	Div's	0.45	$ 13.6		$ 58.80	0.23	30.48	$ 1,509	$ 1,792
7/10/2000	Cash			$ 50	$ 56.45	0.89	31.37	$ 1,559	$ 1,771
9/8/2000	Div's	0.45	$ 14.1		$ 54.12	0.26	31.63	$ 1,573	$ 1,712
9/20/2000	Cash			$ 50	$ 56.43	0.89	32.51	$ 1,623	$ 1,835
11/10/2000	Cash			$ 50	$ 57.53	0.87	33.38	$ 1,673	$ 1,921
12/8/2000	Div's	0.45	$ 14.6		$ 58.63	0.25	33.63	$ 1,688	$ 1,972
	Total		$ 180	$ 1,500					

Susan's 2001, 2002 & 2003 Statement of Accounts

Date	Action	Rate	Div's	Cash	Price	Shares	Total	Basis	Equity
2/10/2001	Cash			$ 50	$ 63.73	0.78	34.42	$ 1,736	$ 2,193
3/9/2001	Div's	0.45	$ 15.49		$ 69.83	0.22	34.64	$ 1,751	$ 2,419
4/20/2001	Cash			$ 50	$ 70.04	0.71	35.36	$ 1,801	$ 2,476
6/8/2001	Div's	0.45	$ 15.91		$ 72.05	0.22	35.58	$ 1,817	$ 2,563
6/20/2001	Cash			$ 50	$ 71.88	0.70	36.27	$ 1,867	$ 2,607
9/10/2001	Div's	0.45	$ 16.32		$ 70.53	0.23	36.50	$ 1,884	$ 2,575
9/10/2001	Cash			$ 50	$ 70.53	0.71	37.21	$ 1,934	$ 2,625
10/10/2001		Name	changed	to	Chevron				
11/27/2001	Cash			$ 46	$ 84.90	0.54	37.75	$ 1,984	$ 3,205
12/10/2001	Div's	0.70	$ 26.41		$ 87.26	0.30	38.06	$ 2,010	$ 3,321
1/20/2002	Cash			$ 46	$ 88.05	0.52	38.58	$ 2,060	$ 3,397
3/11/2002	Div's	0.70	$ 26.98		$ 89.67	0.30	38.88	$ 2,087	$ 3,486
3/19/2002	Cash			$ 46	$ 91.60	0.50	39.38	$ 2,137	$ 3,607
6/10/2002	Div's	0.70	$ 27.55		$ 87.06	0.32	39.70	$ 2,165	$ 3,456
6/10/2002	Cash			$ 46	$ 87.06	0.53	40.22	$ 2,215	$ 3,502
8/16/2002	Cash			$ 46	$ 81.23	0.57	40.79	$ 2,265	$ 3,314
9/10/2002	Div's	0.70	$ 28.53		$ 75.41	0.38	41.17	$ 2,293	$ 3,104
10/10/2002	Cash			$ 46	$ 71.66	0.64	41.81	$ 2,343	$ 2,996
12/10/2002	Div's	0.70	$ 29.25		$ 67.92	0.43	42.24	$ 2,373	$ 2,869
3/10/2003	Div's	0.73	$ 30.84		$ 65.31	0.47	42.71	$ 2,405	$ 2,789
3/10/2003				$ 50.00	$ 65.31	0.77	43.48	$2,455	$ 2,840
5/20/2003	Cash			$ 50.00	$ 69.50	0.72	44.20	$2,505	$ 3,072
6/10/2003	Div's	0.73	$ 32.26		$ 74.32	0.43	44.63	$2,537	$ 3,317
8/10/2003	Cash			$ 50.00	$ 74.53	0.67	45.30	$2,587	$ 3,376
9/10/2003	Div's	0.73	$ 33.07		$ 73.83	0.45	45.75	$2,620	$ 3,378
10/10/2003	Cash			$ 50.00	$ 76.33	0.66	46.41	$2,670	$ 3,542
12/10/2003	Div's	0.73	$ 33.88		$ 78.89	0.43	46.83	$2,704	$ 3,695
12/10/2003	Cash			$ 50.00	$ 76.33	0.66	47.49	$2,754	$ 3,625
	Total		$ 496.5	$ 2,226					

Susan's 2004, 2005 & 2006 Statement of Accounts

Date	Action	Rate	Div's	Cash	Price	Shares	Total	Basis	Equity
5/20/2004	Cash			$ 50.00	$ 90.65	0.55	48.32	$2,889	$ 4,381
6/10/2004	Div's	0.73	$ 35.27		$ 90.80	0.39	48.71	$2,924	$ 4,423
7/10/2004	Cash			$ 50.00	$ 76.33	0.66	49.36	$2,974	$ 3,768
9/10/2004	Div's	0.73	$ 36.04		$ 101.26	0.36	49.72	$3,010	$ 5,035
9/10/2004		Stock	Split		$ 50.63	49.7	99.44	$3,010	$ 5,035
10/10/2004	Cash			$ 50.00	$ 51.76	0.97	100.4	$3,060	$ 5,197
12/10/2004	Div's	0.40	$ 40.16		$ 52.86	0.76	101.2	$3,100	$ 5,348
12/20/2004	Cash			$ 50.00	$ 53.47	0.94	102.1	$3,150	$ 5,459
2/20/2005	Cash			$ 50.00	$ 56.32	0.89	103.0	$3,200	$ 5,800
3/10/2005	Div's	0.45	$ 46.34		$ 59.17	0.78	103.8	$3,247	$ 6,140
4/20/2005	Cash			$ 50.00	$ 53.47	0.94	104.7	$3,297	$ 5,599
6/10/2005	Div's	0.45	$ 47.12		$ 56.13	0.84	105.5	$3,344	$ 5,924
6/20/2005	Cash			$ 50.00	$ 53.47	0.94	106.5	$3,394	$ 5,694
9/12/2005	Div's	0.45	$ 47.92		$ 63.52	0.75	107.2	$3,442	$ 6,811
8/20/2005	Cash			$ 50.00	$ 53.47	0.94	108.2	$3,492	$ 5,784
12/12/2005	Cash			$ 50.00	$ 59.55	0.84	109.0	$3,542	$ 6,492
12/12/2005	Div's	0.45	$ 49.05		$ 59.55	0.82	109.8	$3,591	$ 6,541
1/20/2006	Cash			$ 50.00	$ 56.51	0.88	110.7	$3,641	$ 6,257
3/10/2006	Div's	0.52	$ 57.57		$ 54.39	1.06	111.8	$3,698	$ 6,080
3/20/2006	Cash			$ 50.00	$ 56.24	0.89	112.7	$3,748	$ 6,336
6/12/2006	Div's	0.52	$ 58.59		$ 58.08	1.01	113.7	$3,807	$ 6,602
6/12/2006	Cash			$ 50.00	$ 58.08	0.86	114.5	$3,857	$ 6,652
9/11/2006	Div's	0.52	$ 59.56		$ 61.98	0.96	115.5	$3,917	$ 7,158
9/11/2006	Cash			$ 50.00	$ 61.98	0.81	116.3	$3,967	$ 7,208
10/20/2006	Cash			$ 50.00	$ 65.57	0.76	117.1	$4,017	$ 7,676
12/11/2006	Div's	0.52	$ 60.87		$ 73.03	0.83	117.9	$4,077	$ 8,611
	Total		$ 1,078	$ 3,000					

Appendix 4.

Susan's 2007, 2008 & 2009 Statement of Accounts

Date	Action	Rate	Divi's	Cash	Price	Shares	Total	Basis	Equity
12/29/2006	Cash			$ 50.00	$ 73.03	0.68	118.6	$ 4,487	$ 8,661
3/8/2007	Cash			$ 50.00	$ 69.20	0.72	118.6	$ 4,487	$ 8,207
3/12/2007	Div's	0.52	$ 61.67		$ 68.35	0.90	119.5	$4,549	$ 8,168
5/17/2007	Cash			$ 50.00	$ 80.19	0.62	120.13	$4,599	$ 9,632
6/11/2007	Div's	0.58	$ 69.67		$ 80.95	0.86	120.99	$4,668	$ 9,794
7/26/2007	Cash			$ 50.00	$ 84.27	0.59	121.58	$4,718	$ 10,246
9/10/2007	Div's	0.58	$ 70.52		$ 87.68	0.80	122.38	$4,789	$ 10,731
10/4/2007	Cash			$ 50.00	$ 89.80	0.56	122.94	$4,839	$ 11,040
12/10/2007	Div's	0.58	$ 71.31		$ 91.86	0.78	123.72	$4,910	$ 11,364
12/13/2007	Cash			$ 50.00	$ 92.20	0.54	124.26	$4,960	$ 11,457
2/15/2008	Cash			$ 50.00	$ 91.65	0.55	124.81	$5,010	$ 11,438
3/10/2008	Div's	0.65	$ 80.77		$ 85.80	0.94	124.66	$5,041	$ 10,696
4/25/2008	Cash			$ 50.00	$ 92.70	0.54	125.20	$5,091	$ 11,606
6/10/2008	Div's	0.65	$ 81.38		$ 99.70	0.82	125.62	$5,122	$ 12,524
7/3/2008	Cash			$ 50.00	$ 84.50	0.59	126.21	$5,172	$ 10,665
9/10/2008	Div's	0.65	$ 82.04		$ 80.66	1.02	127.23	$5,254	$ 10,262
9/11/2008	Cash			$ 50.00	$ 82.20	0.61	127.84	$5,304	$ 10,508
11/20/2008	Cash			$ 50.00	$ 72.87	0.69	128.52	$5,354	$ 9,366
12/10/2008	Div's	0.65	$ 83.54		$ 77.50	1.08	129.60	$5,438	$ 10,044
1/29/2009	Cash			$ 50.00	$ 63.50	0.79	130.39	$5,488	$ 8,280
3/10/2009	Div's	0.65	$ 84.75		$ 60.74	1.40	131.79	$5,573	$ 8,005
4/20/2009	Cash			$ 50.00	$ 65.93	0.76	132.54	$5,623	$ 8,739
6/10/2009	Div's	0.65	$ 86.15		$ 60.74	1.42	133.96	$5,709	$ 8,137
6/29/2009	Cash			$ 50.00	$ 66.02	0.76	134.72	$5,759	$ 8,894
9/10/2009	Div's	0.68	$ 93.16		$ 71.35	1.31	136.03	$5,852	$ 9,705
9/23/2009	Cash			$ 50.00	$ 73.53	0.68	136.70	$5,902	$ 10,052
11/10/2009	Cash			$ 50.00	$ 75.62	0.66	137.37	$5,952	$ 10,388
12/10/2009	Div's	0.68	$ 93.41		$ 77.75	1.20	138.57	$6,045	$ 10,774
1/30/2010	Cash			$ 50.00	$ 74.31	0.67	139.24	$6,095	$ 10,347
3/10/2010	Div's	0.68	$ 94.68		$ 73.62	1.29	140.53	$6,190	$ 10,346
	TOTALS		$ 1,259	$ 3,850.00					

Appendix 5.

Susan's 24 year
Dividend and Equity Projections

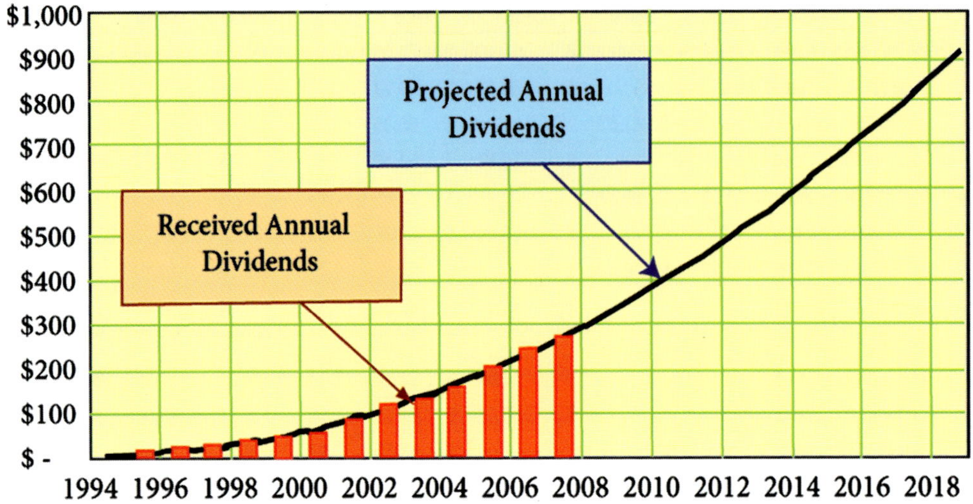

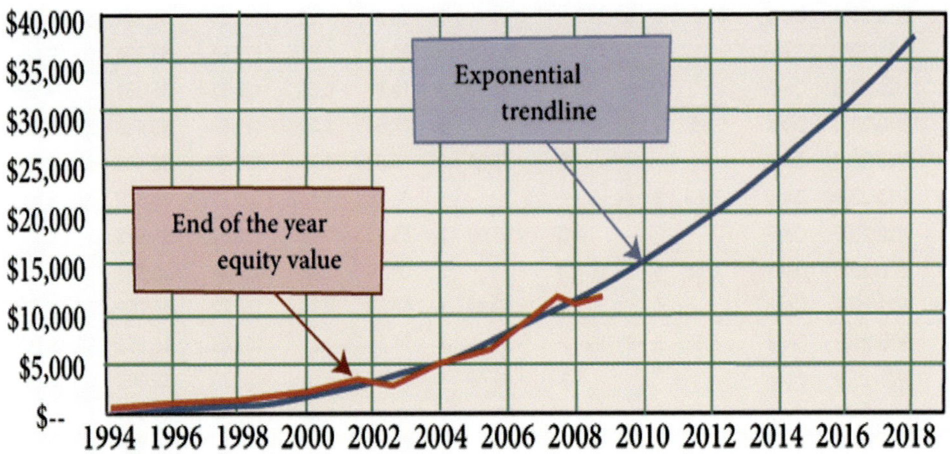

These annual dividends, end of the year equity values and 24 year projections are based on the 1995 to 2009 data published in appendices 3 and 4.

Appendix 6

Nine DRIPs Mentioned in this book

It should not be construed that by listing information about the stocks mentioned in this book, that I am recommending them. They are listed here only to provide you with the information you need to obtain a prospectus. For a qualified recommendation you need to acquire Charles B. Carlson's directory (see page 28).

Atmos Energy
American Stock Transfer & Trust Company
Wall Street Station
PO Box 922, New York NY 10269-0560
1-800-543-3038 or www.amstock.com
Dividends are paid in March, June, September and December.

Chevron Corporation
BNY Mellon Shareowner Services
P.O. Box 358035, Pittsburgh PA 15252-8035
1-800-368-8357 or www.bnymellon.com/shareowner
Dividends are paid in March, June, September and December.

Edison International
Shareowner Services Direct Purchase Plan
PO Box 64856, St. Paul MN 55164-0856
1-800-347-8625 or www.shareowneronline.com
Dividends are paid in February, May, August and November.

General Electric Company
BNY Mellon/General Electric/Shareowner Services
P.O. Box 358035, Pittsburgh PA 15252-8035
1-800-786-2543 or www.bnymellon.com/shareowner
Dividends are paid in January, April, July, and October.

Pepsico, INC.
BNY Mellon Shareowner Services
P.O. Box 358035, Pittsburgh PA 15252-8035
1-800-226-0083 or www.bnymellon.com/shareowner Dividends are paid in March, June, September and December.

Pfizer Inc.
Computershare Trust Company, N.A.
PO Box 43078, Providence RI 02940-3078
1-800-733-9393 or www.computershare.com/investor
Dividends are paid in March, June, September and December.

Pinnacle West Capital Corporation.
BNY Mellon Shareowner Services
P.O. Box 358035, Pittsburgh PA 15252-8035
1-800-457-2983 or www.bnymellon.com/shareowner
Dividends are paid in March, June, September and December.

Popular Inc.
Banco Popular de Puerto Rico
PO Box 362708, San Juan PR 00936-2708
1-877-764-1893 or www.popular.com/Investor Services
Dividends are paid in January, April, July, and October.

Sempra Energy.
American Stock Transfer & Trust Company, LLC.
PO Box 922, Wall Street Station, New York NY 10269-0560
1-877-773-6772 or www.amstock.com
Dividends are paid in January, April, July, and October.

Appendix 7

Create a Permanent Record Template

If you have Microsoft Office on your computer you can design an Excel worksheet template which you can use to create Permanent DRIP records for all of your DRIPs, but first you need a folder in which to hold them.

Your DRIP Portfolio

1. Logo and click the **Start** button.
2. At the top of the Start menu click **My Documents** and the **File and Folders** task menu appears.
3. Click **Make a New Folder**, a New Folder icon appears.
4. Click **Rename this folder**.
5. In the name panel under the New Folder icon change the name to **DRIP Portfolio** then click on a white area to unselect the folder.
6. Click the **DRIP Portfolio** icon with the right mouse button and a sub-menu drops down. Click **Create Shortcut** then select and **move** the shortcut to the **Desktop**.

A Permanent Record Template

1. Double click on the DRIP Portfolio shortcut to open it, then click **File** and then **New**.
2. The Programs menu appears. Double click on the **Microsoft Excel Worksheet** icon. A blank Excel workbook labeled New Excel Worksheet is displayed.
3. On the standard tool bar click **File**, and then **Page Setup**. Click the **Page tab**. Under **Orientation**, select **Landscape**.
4. Click the **Margins** tab and use the spin arrows to set:
   Top, 1.0",
   Bottom 0.6",
   Left and Right 0.6",
   Gutter 0, Gutter position, Left.
5. Click Headers and footers tab and in the Left

Section click on the Date icon, In the Center Section type "**Template.**"

6. Click **Enter,** then type "**Permanent Record Sheet**".
7. Click "**OK**".
8. On the Standard tool bar, click **File**, then **Save As**.
9. In the Save As dialog box for **Save In** enter **DRIP Portfolio**, in **File name** enter **Permanent Record Template** and in **Save as,** navigate to **Microsoft Excel Workbook**.
10. Click "Save."
11. The workbook redisplays with Permanent Record Template in the Title Bar. Rectangles where rows and columns intersect are referred to as cells; each cell has an address formed from the column letter and row number. Data such as formulas, values, dates, labels, numbers and functions are entered in the cells.
12. Use either the mouse, tab or keyboard arrow to select cell **A1,** and enter the label "**Transaction**". The text appears in the cell. If there is insufficient room in the cell for every character, you can either change the font to a smaller size or widen the cell by moving the cursor to the line column line between **A** and **B** until two vertical lines appear, then drag the cell to the right.
13. Use the → to select the **B1** cell, enter "**Dividend**".
14. On the standard tool bar, click, "**Save**".
15. Use the → to select the C**1** cell, enter "**Dividend**".
16. Use the → to select the D**1** cell, enter "**Optional**".
17. Use the → to select the **E1** cell, enter "**Commission**".
18. Use the → to select the **F1** cell, enter "**Basis**".
19. Use the → to select the **G1** cell, enter "**Share**".
20. Use the → to select the **H1** cell, enter "**Shares**".
21. Use the → to select the I**1** cell, enter "**Total**".
22. Use the → to select the **J1** cell, enter "**Equity**".
23. Use the mouse or keyboard arrow to select cell **A2, enter "date".**
24. On the standard tool bar, click, "**Save**".
25. Use the → to select the **B2** cell, enter "**rate**".
26. Use the → to select the **C2** cell, enter "**received**".
27. Use the → to select the D**2** cell, enter "**cash**".
28. Use the → to select the **E2** cell, enter "**& fees**".
29. Use the → to select the F**2** cell, enter "0" (zero)".

30. Use the → to select the **G2** cell, enter "**price**".
31. Use the → to select the **H2** cell, enter "**received**".
32. Use the → to select the **I2** cell, enter "**0**" (zero).
33. Use the → to select the J2 cell, leave it empty.
34. Select cell **F2** and click the "**$**" button on the Formatting tool bar (just below the Standard tool bar).
37. Click "Save."

	A	B	C	D	E	F	G	H	I	J
1	Transaction	Dividend	Dividend	Optional	Commission	Basis	Share	Shares	Total	Equity
2	date	rate	received	cash	& fees	$	price	received	0	$ -
3						$ -				
4										
5										
6										
7										
8										
9										

A Permanent Record Template

Simple calculations are performed in Excel by creating formulas from numbers and cell addresses. When you insert the equal sign, "=" in a cell, Excel understands you are placing a formula in the cell for it to resolve, and places the answer in the cell. Excel uses the "+" sign to perform addition, the "-" sign for subtraction, the "/" sign to perform division and the "*" sign to perform multiplication.

For example, when we enter "=I3*B4" in the C4 cell, we are stating that the product of the values in the I3 cell and the B4 cell results in the C4 cell value.

38. Select cell **C3** and enter, "**=B3*I2**."
39. Select cell **F3** and enter, "**=F2+C3+D3+E3**".
40. Select cell **H3** and enter, "**=(C3+D3)/G3**".
41. Select cell **I3** and enter, "**=I2+H3**".
42. Select cell **J3** and enter, "**=G3*I3**".
43. Click "**Save**."
44. Close the **Permanent Record Template** file.

For Practice you should insert the data from the Pinnacle West PRS on Page 44.

1. Double click on the DRIP Portfolio shortcut to open it, then click Open and then Permanent Record Template.
2. On the Standard tool bar, click File, then Save As.
3. In the Save As dialog box for Save In enter DRIP Portfolio, in File name enter Pinnacle West PRS and Save as, a Microsoft Excel Workbook.
4. Click "Save."
5. Enter 1/31/08 in cell A3, $250 in cell D3 and $38.04 in cell G3. If you inserted the correct formulas in the other cells in row 3, their values should appear. However, should some cells show ####, it means the value is too long for the cell. Either select the cell and either reduce the size of the font or click the Decrease Decimal button on the Formatting tool bar (just below the Standard tool bar).

	A	B	C	D	E	F	G	H	I	J
1	Transaction	Dividend	Dividend	Optional	Commission	Basis	Share	Shares	Total	Equity
2	date	rate	received	cash	& fees	$	price	received	0	
3	1/31/2008			$250.00		$ 250.00	$38.04	6.572	6.572	$250.00
4	3/3/2008	0.525	$3.45			$253.45	$35.06	0.098	6.670	$233.85
5										
6										
7										
8										
9										

A Pinnacle West Permanent Record Sheet

6. Enter the Dividend rate 0.525 in cell B4 and the Share price $35.60 in G4. The $ 3.45 dividends received should automatically appear in cell C4.
7. Select cell F3 and click Copy. Click cell F4 and click Paste. The updated Basis shows the additional $3.45.

8. Drag the cursor across the row of cells H3, I3 and J3, to select them. Click Copy then select the row of cells H4, I4 and J4 and click Paste. The cells are updated to their new values.
9. Click "Save."
10. Close the Pinnacle West PRS file.

It is a good idea to compare the numbers in your Permanent Record Sheet against those printed on the Statement of Account you receive from the company. Sometimes a company will list the prices of a shares held in the plan up to six decimal places and that can cause a discrepancy. Occasionally a company will change the dividend rate which will also result in many differences.

Appendix 8

Qualified Dividends & Capital Gain Worksheet

Form 1040—Line 44

Qualified Dividends and Capital Gain Tax Worksheet—Line 44 *Keep for Your Records*

Before you begin:
- √ See the instructions for line 44 that begin on page 37 to see if you can use this worksheet to figure your tax.
- √ If you do not have to file Schedule D and you received capital gain distributions, be sure you checked the box on line 13 of Form 1040.

1. Enter the amount from Form 1040, line 43. However, if you are filing Form 2555 or 2555-EZ (relating to foreign earned income), enter the amount from line 3 of the worksheet on page 38 . . . . **1.** ______

2. Enter the amount from Form 1040, line 9b* . . . . **2.** ______

3. Are you filing Schedule D?*

☐ **Yes.** Enter the **smaller** of line 15 or 16 of Schedule D. If either line 15 or line 16 is a loss, enter -0-

☐ **No.** Enter the amount from Form 1040, line 13 } **3.** ______

4. Add lines 2 and 3 . . . . **4.** ______

5. If you are claiming investment interest expense on Form 4952, enter the amount from line 4g of that form. Otherwise, enter -0- . . . . **5.** ______

6. Subtract line 5 from line 4. If zero or less, enter -0- . . . . **6.** ______

7. Subtract line 6 from line 1. If zero or less, enter -0- . . . . **7.** ______

8. Enter the **smaller** of:
- The amount on line 1, or
- $33,950 if single or married filing separately, $67,900 if married filing jointly or qualifying widow(er), $45,500 if head of household.

} . . . . **8.** ______

9. Is the amount on line 7 equal to or more than the amount on line 8?

☐ **Yes.** Skip lines 9 and 10; go to line 11 and check the "No" box.

☐ **No.** Enter the amount from line 7 . . . . **9.** ______

10. Subtract line 9 from line 8 . . . . **10.** ______

11. Are the amounts on lines 6 and 10 the same?

☐ **Yes.** Skip lines 11 through 14; go to line 15.

☐ **No.** Enter the **smaller** of line 1 or line 6 . . . . **11.** ______

12. Enter the amount from line 10 (if line 10 is blank, enter -0-) . . . . **12.** ______

13. Subtract line 12 from line 11 . . . . **13.** ______

14. Multiply line 13 by 15% (.15) . . . . **14.** ______

15. Figure the tax on the amount on line 7. Use the Tax Table or Tax Computation Worksheet, whichever applies . . . . **15.** ______

16. Add lines 14 and 15 . . . . **16.** ______

17. Figure the tax on the amount on line 1. Use the Tax Table or Tax Computation Worksheet, whichever applies . . . . **17.** ______

18. **Tax on all taxable income.** Enter the **smaller** of line 16 or line 17. Also include this amount on Form 1040, line 44. If you are filing Form 2555 or 2555-EZ, do not enter this amount on Form 1040, line 44. Instead, enter it on line 4 of the worksheet on page 38 . . . . **18.** ______

**If you are filing Form 2555 or 2555-EZ, see the footnote in the worksheet on page 38 before completing this line.*

Qualified Dividends & Capital Gain Worksheets are published in Form 1040 Instructions along with easy to understand directions.

Appendix 9

Portfolio Tracking Workbook

If you used an Excel program to create a Permanent Record Sheet, you can use the same skills to create a Portfolio Tracking Workbook which makes tracking, comparing and rebalancing your DRIPS a breeze.

1. Logon and click the Start button.
2. Double click on Drip portfolio shortcut icon to open the folder.
3. Click File, then New. The Programs menu appears.
4. Double click the Microsoft Excel Worksheet icon to open a blank Excel workbook labeled New Excel Worksheet.
5. Click File on the standard tool bar and then Page Setup.
6. Click the Margins tab, set Top, 1.0", Bottom, 0.6", Left, 0.6", Right 0.6", Gutter, 0, Gutter position, Left, Under Orientation, select Landscape.
7. Click the Layout tab, under Headers & footers, set Headers
   0.5" and Footers 0.5". Set Vertical Alignment to Top.
8. Click OK.
9. On the Standard tool bar, click File, then Save As.
10. In the Save In box, navigate to DRIP portfolio.
11. In File name, enter 2009 (or present year) Portfolio.
12. In Save as, navigate to Microsoft Excel Workbook.
13. Click Save.
14. The workbook redisplays with the 2009 Portfolio label.
15. Click on the A1 cell to select it and enter Name.
16. Use the → to select the B1 cell, enter Qty.
17. Use the → to select the C1 cell, enter Rate.
18. Use the → to select the D1 cell, enter Price.
19. Use the → to select the E1 cell, enter Basis.
20. Use the → to select the F1 cell, enter Dividend.
21. Use the → to select the G1 cell, enter Dividend.
22. Use the → to select the H1 cell, enter Dividend.
23. Use the → to select the I1 cell, enter Yield.
24. Use the → to select the J1 cell, enter 2009 or the current year.
25. Use the → to select the K1 cell , enter Value.
26. Click Save.
27. Continue by entering text labels listing the months

dividend payments are made. In the F2 cell enter 1/4/7/10, → in the G2 cell enter 2/5/8/11 and in the H2 cell enter 3/6/9/12.

28. In the J2 cell, enter Dividends.

Use your keyboard to enter formulas; use = for equals, use + for add, - for subtract, / for divide and * for multiply. Remember, when you enter a formula in a cell, nothing is displayed unless there are values in the referenced cells.

29. Start by placing formulas in row three by entering the formula for percentage yield in cell I3. Percentage yield is usually obtained by multiplying the annual dividend by 100 and dividing by the market price of the stock, which would make the formula, 400* C3/D3. However, after several months the market price of the stock will be quite different to the amount you paid for it, to obtain a truer price, rearrange the equation for quantity of stock you purchase, Qty = Basis/Price, which is D3' = E3/B3. Substitute D3' for D3 in the formula for yield and it becomes 400*C3*(B3/E3).

30. Enter =400*C3*(B3/E) in cell I3.
31. Enter =(F3+G3+H3)*4 in cell J3 to display the total dividends you expect to receive in 2009.
32. Enter =B3*D3 in cell K3 to display the current value of your stock.
33. Enter =J6/B6 in cell I6 to display your portfolio yield.
34. Select the cells in column I from I3 to the bottom of the sheet and click the % button on the Standard Tool bar.
35. Click Save.
36. Click View in the Standard Tool bar and select Headers and Footers. Click Custom Header. Choose Center Section and enter 2009 Portfolio Tracking, or whatever is your choice for your workbook's name.
37. Click OK twice.
38. Leave three rows empty and enter TOTALS in cell A6.
39. Click on cell B6 to select it and enter =SUM(B3:B5).
40. Click on cell B6 to select it and click Copy.
41. Hold down Ctrl and dray the cursor across cells E6, F6, G6, H6, J6, K6, L6 and M6 to select them.
42. Click Paste to insert the formula.
43. Hold down the Ctrl key and drag the cursor down columns C, D, E, F, G, H, I, J, K and L to select them, 44.

Cick the $ button on the Standard tool bar.

43. Click Save.

For practice, enter the data for a person who began a portfolio by putting $1,000 in three different DRIPS; Chevron Corp., Pfizer Inc., and Popular Inc., with stock prices of $73.03, $24.855 and $18.646 and dividend rates of 0.52, 0.24 and 0.16 respectively.

Your portfolio tracking worksheet should be similar to that below.

	A	B	C	D	E	F	G	H	I	J	K
1	Name	Qty.	Rate	Price	Basis	Dividend	Dividend	Dividend	Yield	2009	Value
2						1/4/7/10	2/5/8/11	3/6/9/12		Dividend	
3	Chevron	13.69	0.53	$73.03	$1,000	$ 7.12			2.8%	$ 28.48	$1,000
4	Pfizer	40.23	0.24	$24.86	$1,000		$ 9.66		3.9%	$ 38.64	$1,000
5	Popular	53.63	0.16	$18.65	$1,000			$ 8.58	3.4%	$ 34.32	$1,000
6	TOTALS	108			$3,000	$ 7.12	$ 9.66	$ 8.58	3.4%	$ 101.44	$3,000

December 12, 2006 Portfolio Tracking Worksheet

The advantages of using a Portfolio Tracking Worksheet can be seen when after twelve months the number of stock, rates, market prices of the same three companies were entered into an updated worksheet. Oil companies did very well in and the folder **2007, as can be seen by Chevron's 30% increase in value, the drug company Pfizer did Okay by losing only 16% while producing a higher yield.**

	A	B	C	D	E	F	G	H	I	J	K
1	Name	Qty.	Rate	Price	Basis	Dividend	Dividend	Dividend	Yield	2009	Value
2						1/4/7/10	2/5/8/11	3/6/9/12		Dividend	
3	Chevron	14.10	0.58	$91.96	$1,029	$ 8.18			2.5%	$ 32.71	$1,297
4	Pfizer	41.80	0.29	$23.54	$1,039		$ 12.12		4.9%	$ 48'49	$984
5	Popular	55.47	0.16	$9.914	$1,034			$ 8.88	6.5%	$ 35.50	$550
6	TOTALS	111			$3,102	$ 8.18	$ 12.12	$ 8.88	3.8%	$ 116.7	$2,831

December 4, 2007 Portfolio Tracking Worksheet

Index

Make a copy of this Order Form

Money Orders, checks to *Fantastik-Act Publishing*, PO Box 2096, Lynnwood, WA 98036-2095

Please send the following books;

"*Learn How to Build Your Treasure Chest Sail to a Safe Harbor and Financial Security*"

Price $15.95 each. With the exception of autographed books, I understand that I may return a clean book, within 21 days for a full refund.

Number of books desired ☐ at $15.95.........$.........

Shipping: U.S. $5.00 for first book and $2.00 for each additional book..................................$..........

Sales Tax: Please add the appropiate sales tax for books plus shipping, sent to a Washington State address, Typically 9.5%.........................$...........

Total enclosed:.........$..........

Please include a free catalogue of Giglee fine-art reproductions of paintings by Reginald Allen ☐

Please autograph my book(s) with the message on the back of this order form or on a sheet of paper. ☐

Name...

Address...

City..

State..**Zip**...................

Telephone...

Email..